Death of a
Marketer

Death of a
Marketer

of a

Andrea Fryrear

MODERN MARKETING'S TROUBLED PAST AND
A NEW APPROACH TO CHANGE THE FUTURE

Death of a Marketer:
Modern Marketing's Troubled Past
and a New Approach to Change the Future

Published by Corsac Publishing
Longmont, Colorado

Library of Congress Control Number: 2017902462
Fryrear, Andrea, Author
Death of a Marketer:
Modern Marketing's Troubled Past and a New Approach to Change the Future
Andrea Fryrear

ISBN: 978-0-9987211-0-1
BUS043000 **BUSINESS & ECONOMICS** / Marketing / General

QUANTITY PURCHASES: Schools, companies, professional groups, clubs, and other organizations may qualify for special terms when ordering quantities of this title. For information, email Corsac Publishing at info@corsacpublishing.com.

Corsac Publishing

Praise for *Death of a Marketer*

"It has saddened me to see so many marketers in the world destroying themselves with outdated processes, poor workflow and an overall dated approach to marketing strategy. My wish is to go back to each and every one of them I've encountered along the way and give them this book. It's a sanity saver!"

— Joe Pulizzi, Founder, Content Marketing Institute
Best-selling author of four books including
Content Inc. and *Epic Content Marketing*

"If you want to cut through the noise of what Agile Marketing really is, and how it can help you evolve your marketing into the next era — you need to open this book and start dog-earing every other page. With this book, Andrea has accomplished nothing short of injecting joy, passion and true strategy into our beloved practice of marketing."

— Robert Rose, Chief Strategy Advisor,
Content Marketing Institute

"A beautifully written guide to taming the chaos and complexity of modern marketing through agile management principles and practices."

— Scott Brinker, Author, *Hacking Marketing*

"In the advice-giving era, where everyone has their One Way to promote, Andrea's is a refreshing approach: a smart look at multiple methodologies, analyzed and distilled, so you can better execute in your own specific context and succeed. This is THE jumping off point to make agile marketing work for you."

— Jay Acunzo, creator and host, Unthinkable podcast

"*Death of a Marketer* is both a well-written history of marketing and a prescription for improving the future of the profession. It introduces the four major methodologies of Agile Marketing and provides some wonderful guidance on the strengths and limits of each. Highly recommended."

— Jim Ewel, Blogger, AgileMarketing.net

"The best marketers know they need to adapt constantly and continuously improve how they engage and connect with fragmented target markets; the challenge is in how to do so well. In *Death of a Marketer*, Fryrear shows us how an agile approach will resurrect marketing as a true company asset, fully armed and ready to create and sustain competitive advantages in real-time."

— Ardath Albee, author, *Digital Relevance: Developing Marketing Content and Strategies that Drive Results*

"More than any other book to date, *Death of a Marketer* accurately describes marketing's challenges with digital transformation and how marketers can overcome those challenges with Agile Marketing."

— John Cass, Boston Agile Marketing Meetup Co-Founder & SprintZero 2012 Chair

"Andrea takes the assumption that marketers can't know everything up front, and with that assumption makes a compelling case for a shift to an Agile marketing approach. Her book gives insight into how marketers arrived at the current state of less-than-effective marketing and shares a well-thought-out plan for a better, more adaptable way forward."

— Joe Staples, Chief Marketing Officer, Workfront

"Andrea Fryrear has nailed it! *Death of a Marketer* brilliantly illustrates the problem marketers have with truly moving our profession forward with creativity and innovation. We're tethered to the past - continually reworking outdated processes - rather than exploring new ways of creating value for brands, customers and employees. Her Agile approach to marketing gives readers both the vision and know-how to step off the hamster wheel and step onto the fast-track. A must-read for every marketer who wants to stop talking about value and start creating it."

— Carla Johnson, Keynote speaker, author, storyteller and creative explorer, Type A Communications

For Dan, who meets me where I am
and helps me go someplace better.
I am the luckiest.

Table of Contents

Foreword

"There's a way to do it better -- find it."
Thomas A. Edison

When Nietzsche announced that "God is dead" at the dawn of our modern age, he was essentially placing the power to shape the own world in our own hands. Today, the business "creatives" of marketing, the corporate messengers, and the spin-masters have yielded that power to the customer. The almighty consumers are ascendant, and with supercomputers in their hands they have become smarter and more sophisticated, constantly raising the bar of their expectations for digital content.

And so, in order to survive, marketing has evolved. We're now participants in conversations, not sources of truth. But where does that leave our profession? Are we obsolete, suddenly nonexistent?

No, marketing is just as essential and influential as it ever was. But to join the changing digital conversation it's had to go through its own cycle of death and rebirth—a process that we are still engaged in right now.

For 150 years we have been ignoring the declining effectiveness of traditional tactics. But we can no longer run away from the tough realization that to succeed at modern marketing we have to sell, without selling anything, and still prove to our boss that it's working.

We have to set aside old school approaches and seek to be simultaneously relevant to our customers and impactful to our business.

Luckily for us, we can do this with Agile marketing.

Agile is not a buzzword. It is not the latest "shiny object" marketing technique. It is not a cut-and-paste template that you can use to hit the mark with your next marketing campaign.

It is an approach. A mindset. A way of thinking and doing and being. It's not something we can hold in our hands.

And yet it is something that will help our entire industry achieve the promise of marketing: To attract and retain customers. To drive product innovations. To build memorable customer experiences that lead to higher sales, profits, and long-term value.

In this book, Andrea Fryrear is giving us a gift. A gift for the craft that I love – a love that, if you are reading this right now, we most certainly share. It's time to step into the Agile process, to transform what being a marketer means, and through that, return to the essence of our job – telling the story of our world as it unfolds.

Marketing has gone through the pioneering energy of print, the communal appeal of radio, the glamour of television, and the massive disruption of digital. And with every new suit we have put on, we did our best version of the job at that point in time. We informed, entertained, tantalized, and, eventually, saturated. But always we grabbed attention and moved mountains for the brands that we spoke for.

The modern marketer, however, has a different boss.

It is our job to create solutions for the customer, not the company. We have always been the glue that holds the two together, but now the glue is sticking the other way. This means that marketers today can no longer project our old habits into the latest content distribution channels and expect to get results.

We can't just expect our captive audiences to ingest our cues and make the appropriate purchases until we wear out our welcome, and then wait for the next mediums to infiltrate and trends to follow. Our briefcase of marketing tricks and chicanery has to go. And, we don't simply get to pick up a new one this time like we have with every other major shift in platforms and channels.

Today, we carry nothing. No more bag of tricks, no framework to hold onto, nothing to grasp for security and direction.

It's both liberating and terrifying at the same time, isn't it?

What we *do* have with Agile marketing is a new way of thinking and doing and being. It's not be a pre-fabricated briefcase we can pick up and run with. It's something much more exciting.

As we get over the fear and into the freedom, we will see that this death and rebirth of marketing has taken the lid off the paint and handed us a blank canvas. With Agile marketing, we can do anything. We can create the value that every modern executive craves, and we can tap into the joy and passion of doing our best work.

Right now, we work in a time in which the customer is constantly changing. There are infinite niche markets and marketing channels. The rules are constantly being redefined, which is a polite way of saying, there are no rules. The marketing teams that are embracing this uncertainty and who have already become Agile are capable of creating quantifiable results. They are wowing the C-suite, educating and entertaining customers. They are telling the story of today – and it is working.

At my last three companies, I've witnessed Agile marketing techniques move from a cool idea to a considered approach to a cultural commitment. And the results of that commitment paid off.

As an executive at marketing technology startup NewsCred, our marketers followed the lead of our engineers in identifying the high-value projects that would deliver results. They worked in the Scrum method of prioritizing projects in 2-3 week sprints and held daily Standup meetings to discuss progress. They used a Trello board to track results, and most importantly, took the time to discuss what worked and didn't.

We adapted our tactics based on the top search terms, best articles, and highest performing lead generation tactics to effectively tailor our digital and event marketing. What was promoted on Tuesday was often entirely different to what was featured on Thursday.

This is totally unlike traditional, well-planned marketing campaigns, and it is Agile to the core. It is 100 percent responsive.

Having seen first hand Agile marketing go from an interesting idea, to something to consider, and finally to a commitment, I was forever convinced that Agile marketing is like the famous quote from Yoda: "Do. Or do not. There is no try."

Agile is smart, responsive, and remarkably effective in the reality of today's business environment where our customers' attention is fleeting. But our business's financial demands are constant and increasing. Agile marketing is all about paying attention to what the demands are right now, creating a plan, and then constantly reassessing and evolving as needed.

And yes, this implies that it's alright to fail. No marketer can afford to wait for perfect. We must put action behind the best ideas, be willing to learn as we go, and celebrate our failures for the insights they provide. Some things we do won't work out, but our actions are based on analysis and measurement, not theory. And the creativity that Agile empowers is every marketing team's wild card.

Agile marketing is a methodology that must be applied to the day-to-day activities of all marketers if we want to survive. We are relinquishing the old notion that we have control over our marketing and our messaging, and we are replacing that idea with an evolved mindset. This Agile mindset has the power to create an infinite number of solutions to respond to the endlessly shifting demands of the consumer. In a sense, we are admitting that we don't know the answers right now. And we are creating opportunities for listening to our customers and the market telling us what they want.

That is why Agile marketing represents the rebirth of marketing.

Agile is the only thing that will work in a reality that has become formless, infinite, and totally unpredictable.

It's not easy. It will definitely push the boundaries of our own minds and our imaginations. But it will help us make sense of this seemingly chaotic environment that we need to engage.

And it will take a lot of the frustration out of modern marketing.

Learning the Agile approach will help us become as fluid as the digital era demands. It will help us to be successful, but it will also reconnect us to the meaning and purpose of our job in the first place.

We can be flexible, crafting strategies based on now that can then seamlessly adapt to what's next. We can create transparent, liquid workflows that can shift and morph. Our work itself can be straightforward, clean, and effective.

We can be the solution that today's customer is searching for, and the hero that our executives have longed for.

This book is important because Agile marketing has completely revolutionized the way we view marketing as a profession and (hopefully) as a passion. In this book, Andrea will certainly teach you the meaty stuff of what agile is all about. She'll go over the four major methodologies – Scrum, Kanban, Scrumban, and Lean – and she will set you up to determine the best way for your team to become Agile.

But before that, we need to understand where we came from. That's why Andrea begins where I begin every one of my keynotes on marketing – with a look at back the storied history of where marketing has been. To consider what marketing really should be. And then to consider where marketing is going.

It's a wild ride, but I know you're going to love it. Are you ready to be Agile?

- Michael Brenner
Keynote Speaker, Author,
and CEO of Marketing Insider Group

Introduction

"By its nature concerned with the present and future tenses, advertising has no historical memory. Cycles in art and copy styles reappear with new names to be greeted as innovations. Among observers of the American scene, discussions of advertising in our national life always lack a historical dimension." Stephen Fox, *The Mirror Makers*[1]

Leonard Shelby, the protagonist of the 2000 psychological thriller *Memento*, has a problem: as a result of a brain trauma, his memory resets every five minutes. He lives in 300-second intervals, each one unconnected from its predecessors. Despite this significant handicap, he sets out on a single-minded mission to avenge his wife's death. To make up for his lack of long-term memory, Leonard lays a trail of clues that he can retrace following each memory reset. He gets tattoos, takes Polaroid pictures, and obsessively tells and retells the story of a man named Sammy who suffered from the same form of amnesia. Leonard, though, turns out to be an unreliable trail-layer. Realizing that he can't beat his condition, he decides to exploit it by deliberately creating a false path that his future amnesiac self will blindly follow.

Marketers in the twenty-first century have a similar problem.

As a result of decades of continual disruption in our industry, our long-term memory seems to have malfunctioned. Disconnected from the lessons of our past, we search our surroundings for clues on how to succeed in a fragmented present and an uncertain future. But like Leonard Shelby's, our breadcrumb trail isn't completely reliable. Ignorance of the past makes it virtually impossible to fully understand the present or to make meaningful predictions about the course of the future.

Take the iconic chase scene from *Memento*. Half of the movie's plot, the part that deals with Leonard's hunt for his wife's killer, works backward, so that viewers learn in five-minute increments just as Leonard does. This scene takes place in that mode, and when it begins, Leonard is sprinting, mid-stride. His internal monologue begins, "OK. So, what am I doing?" He spots another runner and concludes, "I'm chasing this guy." He veers towards the man, only to realize, "Nope. He's chasing me."

Every quarter, every week, or maybe even every day, marketers likewise walk into their offices and ask themselves, "OK. So, what am I doing?"

We veer first one way, then another, hoping to figure out where we're supposed to be running and why, but whatever else happens, we can't stop running. There are social media feeds to fill, blog posts to write, email automations to queue up, and, of course, meetings to attend.

When the future is closing in at top speed, who has time for a good look at the past?

Like Leonard, who reviews his jumble of Polaroid pictures and redacted police reports every time his memory resets, marketers take a cursory glance at last quarter's numbers and the first few results of a quick Google search and charge ahead. We aren't just ill-informed by being unmoored from the past; our initial *lack* of information rapidly becomes *mis*information, leading us, again and again, like Leonard, down the wrong path.

The closing scene of *Memento* shows Leonard deliberately leaving himself a false trail that will lead to his taking revenge on a man who he knows is not his wife's killer. He resorts to exploiting his short-term focus to manipulate—and ultimately rationalize—his future actions. He remembers nothing; his actions are, with absurd consequences, disconnected from past events.

With no understanding of where we've been, we marketers likewise act haphazardly, scrambling from one tactic to the next in a way that seems, to our audience, to disregard all that came before.

It's not working.

Marketing hasn't suffered a brain trauma; we can fix our amnesia and repair relationships with our audiences. We can know whom we're chasing, why we're chasing them, and how to catch them.

My goal in this book is to convince you that Agile marketing is the way to achieve these goals. For those unfamiliar with the concept, Agile marketing is not just about moving faster or responding instantly. It's a specific, structured way of executing a marketing strategy that focuses on releasing small pieces of work regularly, giving marketers more autonomy in how they execute projects, and getting all the team's processes out in the open so they can be continuously improved.

You'll see me refer to it using a capital "A" in this book, and that's a deliberate choice. "Agile" is often confused with "agile," meaning responsive, adaptive, or nimble, and while these are all excellent things for a marketing department to be, they aren't the same as adopting a specific Agile methodology like Scrum or Kanban. When

I use the phrase "Agile marketing" I'm referring to the practice of deliberately managing the day-to-day work of a group of marketers using Agile principles and values.

This distinction is essential, because while becoming more nimble or responsive might help you get better results for a little while, Agile marketing is what *every* modern marketing team needs to succeed, excel, and keep its members sane over the long term.

Beyond making that case, I want to give you the tools to implement Agile on your team. We all need blueprints to follow, and bad examples to *not* follow, which is partly why the first half of this book lays down a detailed history of marketing. When it comes time to erect our own Agile team, we'll all do something a little different. Prescriptive formulas just don't jive with the varied landscape of marketing teams out there. That's why the final part of this book outlines four distinct Agile methodologies in the hope that you'll find the right one (or the right combination of several) for your unique situation.

Another reason that I feel compelled to relate marketing's history is to overcome the inertia that governs our daily professional lives. Humans are creatures of habit; today's behavior tends to match yesterday's, and last week's, and so on. Change—the real, significant, lasting organizational change that comes from an Agile transformation—is hard. To convince you to make that change, I must first make the case that your current situation has evolved to a point where traditional approaches no longer work. For that, I need history.

Finally, we marketers in particular need to take time to understand our roots, because it's not just our audience's relationship with our brand that impacts how people feel about our work. Their broad, ongoing, tumultuous relationship with marketing and advertising plays a major part in their responses, and it, in turn, has been shaped by short- and long-term history. People have *feelings* about marketing that we must contend with. It's a bonus if, while convincing you that Agile marketing is the next step in marketing's evolution, I can also provide insight into that particular marketing challenge.

Marketing's present may be almost entirely digital, but this transition happened very recently. The roots of marketing's problems and power run deeper than the Internet and social media. We'll see examples of influencer marketing and content marketing from hundreds of years ago that illustrate clearly how much we could learn from our analog predecessors. At the same time, differences between modern marketing and its forebears cannot be overlooked. While the "what" of marketing may be more stable than we realize, the "how" of previous decades no longer applies. A broader perspective can lead only to better marketing.

To get us from patent medicine and handbills through cord-cutting and conflict with the C-suite and finally to the Agile solutions that offer a way forward, this book is structured as follows:

- Part One is devoted to this historical perspective, taking us from the invention of the printing press through the arrival of online video. Since advertising was the most visible and well-documented component of marketing before the digital revolution, it gets the lion's share of coverage here. You could skip this part if you're eager to get to the present and future bits, but, as I hope you learned from the story of Leonard Shelby, the past is powerful.

- Part Two deals with marketing in the digital age, following marketing tactics from Part One to their modern incarnations. From increasing audience fragmentation to battles with the C-suite to the rise of the gig economy, we see how the trends our predecessors initiated brought us to our present predicament.

- Part Three gets to the exciting question of what to do next. Based on the modern situation and its historical antecedents, I argue that adopting Agile marketing principles and practices offers the best path forward. They help individual marketers produce more effective marketing campaigns without being overworked and overwhelmed, and they represent the culmination of the decades-long journey described in Parts One and Two.

I wrote this book as both a thank-you note and a call to action. Several years ago, Agile marketing saved my sanity, and now I want to pay it forward. I talk, write, teach, and read about Agile marketing constantly, and there's more to say than this one book could hold. I see a problem proliferating in marketing and found a solution that worked amazingly well for me, for my team, and for hundreds of marketers that I've spoken with. If I know all this and don't tell anyone about it, I'm culpable in the slow, wasting death of the joy that marketers once found in their work, not to mention the reduced success of marketing teams, declining results for organizations, and the decay of the profession.

I've been where many marketers are today: wandering the digital desert, lips parched and limbs weak, looking for something better. Agile marketing saved me, and I want to offer you a sip from the same well. It might just save you too.

PART ONE

A Brief History of Marketers
Ruining Everything

"Until recently, traditional marketing was nothing but a one-sided boxing match, with businesses slamming right hooks onto the same three or four platforms -- radio, television, print, outdoor, and then later, the Internet -- as fast and as often as possible. It was an unfair fight, but it worked." Gary Vaynerchuk, *Jab, Jab, Jab, Right Hook*

When a new social network comes along, marketers are rarely the first in line to sign up (at least not with our corporate email addresses). We may be early adopters in our personal lives, but professionally, we prefer a safe bet over an exciting gamble. Once the party is in full swing, we show up uninvited and without a gift, tracking mud on the carpet and dancing on tables to get everyone's attention. We're the world's worst guests, which makes people distrustful of everything we say and do.

When you're in the business of persuading people to take action (click this button, opt in to this newsletter, buy this product), entering the conversation with a trust deficit is a problem.

Of course, this bull-in-a-China shop behavior isn't unique to social media. Advertisers and marketers have been barging into living rooms and airwaves and browser windows for decades, which helped establish a trust deficit in the first place. From the moment it became possible to crank out a handbill, entrepreneurs plastered poles and fences with ads. When more portable media like newspapers and magazines came along, fledgling ad agencies were hot on their heels, eager to establish a symbiosis that would inextricably link ads with the printed word. Then came radio, and in the United States at least, advertisers were once again instantly on the scene, helpfully offering sponsorships as a means of bringing education, edification, and entertainment into every living room. (In exchange for which we ask only a moment to tell you about an exciting new product that cures headaches, cleans dishes, and peels potatoes.)

When television then flickered to life, advertisers could hardly believe their good luck. An invention had arrived that would deliver their messages in irresistible packages that arrested the audience's attention completely. This powerful new medium had the potential to change everything: how brands defined themselves, how advertisers ran their businesses, and how consumers engaged with content. Already positioned as the benefactors of radio audiences, advertisers knew how to bring TV viewers the programming they craved, complete with ads interspersed among the laughs and learning.

It all sounds sweet and symbiotic in the abstract, but in every case—printed handbills, newspapers, magazines, radio, television, and digital media—we advertisers and marketers have eventually worn out our welcome. In our (mostly) legitimate attempts to drive sales for our clients and employers, we've abandoned concern for the audience. It's a cycle that has repeated for nearly 150 years, and one that has proven itself as magnetic as a black hole.

Much has been written about *how* marketers mess things up, and we'll tour that soon. Certainly marketers have been boorish in their recent behavior on social media, but *why* do we act this way? It's definitely not because these activity patterns are effective; they alienate audiences rather than establish relationships between them and the brands we serve. Instead, I believe that modern-day marketers insist on barging into every emerging communication channel for three reasons:

1. **Fragmentation of Audience Attention.** The astonishing proliferation of media options and channels (Internet, email, social media, TV, radio, niche magazines, podcasts, and so on) has made us desperate to reach people at any kind of scale. Constantly on the hunt for new prospects, we run around the halls of media sticking our heads in doors yelling, "Anybody in here want to buy this thing?" waiting two seconds, and then slamming the door behind us before running to the next one. People love that, by the way. It's a very effective marketing tactic.

2. **Executive Expectations.** Despite the ongoing skepticism that many marketers face when trying to convince members of upper management that social media marketing is both legitimate and effective, our bosses expect us to hawk our wares anywhere and everywhere. They might still scoff at Twitter, but when they hear about a competitor who had its own filter on Snapchat at last week's trade show, they want to know why we didn't do that (even if they don't quite know what "that" was).

3. **The Lure of Overnight Success.** The history of our profession is hundreds of wild success stories juxtaposed with millions of cautionary tales. We constantly hear, "Don't be like that brand that ignored radio ads and then

went out of business in two days," or, "The first brands on YouTube are now worth a hundred billion dollars." These stories—exaggerations and exceptions, mostly—make us fearful simultaneously of missing the next success story and starring in the next cautionary tale.

Understanding where we came from can give us a better grasp on why we're in this muddle and how to escape it. The next three chapters provide a short history of marketers ruining everything, give us insights into how we became the way we are, and show that there is, in fact, hope.

Many of the anecdotes that I share in this section pertain to advertising. While this is now only one slice (and not even the largest) of the marketing pie, it was once the prime focus of brand marketing. This status, combined with its impact on the emergence of American consumer culture, has made advertising the most visible and best-documented component of marketing's history. Even in modern parlance, mentions of "marketing" are "most regularly used to refer to sales and advertising practices and with little recognition that marketers take account of consumer needs."[2] Many people still conflate advertising and marketing.

For these reasons, Chapters One and Two deal with advertising, specifically as practiced by agencies. We journey through advertising's relationship with print—newspapers and magazines—to how it meshes with radio and television. My motives for taking this leisurely amble through marketing history? To better understand where we came from so that I can identify patterns and themes that point to insights for improving the lives of modern marketers with Agile marketing.

These early chapters also tease out some details about how marketers and advertisers were perceived as professionals, both by themselves and in American culture. Tracking the development of marketing's public image enables us to better manage our new public-relations efforts as more Agile marketers. As we meet early practitioners of the advertising profession, it's worth remembering that "Ads and commercials reflect, to a greater extent than most business products, the quirks and personalities of the people behind them."[3] When we arrive at discussions of team dynamics in Part Three, remember the impact that individual characters will have on your marketing department's output.

This knowledge alone can't break the cycle of innovation and indiscretion and lead us unencumbered into a bright new future. It can, though, help us elevate our current turn in the cycle.

CHAPTER ONE

Print, Radio, and the Attention Barter System

"If advertising persuades some men to live beyond their means, so does matrimony. If advertising speaks to a thousand in order to influence one, so does the church. If advertising is often garrulous and redundant and tiresome, so is the United States Senate. We are young, and law and medicine and theology are old." - Bruce Barton*

Had it come alone, the arrival of the printing press would have made a major impact on marketing. But the technology that made large-scale book production possible helped set in motion the larger Industrial Revolution that ushered in the era of mass production. This double whammy meant that not only could the makers of products communicate with potential customers more cheaply and on a larger scale than ever before; they could also manufacture more physical goods than they could ever have made by hand.

Before the earliest printing presses, all writing was done by hand, and any copies were also created by hand. The earliest printing

---

* Barton was one of the original founders of the advertising agency Barton, Durstine, and Osborn (BDO), which would eventually become BBDO. It remains one of the premier agencies in the world.

presses used woodblocks, which allowed for faster printing than hand copying, but still required a unique woodblock for each page. Woodblocks also tended to survive only a few uses before the copies they produced became illegible. Books were enormously expensive luxuries and magazines were unheard of.

Johannes Gutenberg created his novel printing press in 1447. His use of moveable type—individual letters that could be rearranged to produce any combination of words on a page—freed the written word forever. It eliminated the need to create an exact reproduction of each page in order to produce copies, and the durable metal alloys used to produce the movable type letters could be used over hundreds of printings with no loss in quality.

Once printing had been thus democratized, it took almost no time at all for entrepreneurs to exploit it.

By 1472, the first poster ad in English was put on church doors in London—a smart move by an early advertiser, since just about everybody went to church at least once a week. Since that day, marketers haven't stopped looking for ways to put content in front of as many eyeballs as possible at the lowest cost possible. But advertising would soon move from standalone handbills to its first symbiotic relationship with mass media, because newspapers and magazines were preparing to join the publishing fray.

The Co-Evolution of Newspapers, Magazines, and Advertising

In 1631, Theophraste Renaudot, a French doctor and journalist, created the first French newspaper. At the age of 20, (because he was considered too young to practice medicine) he began to travel across Europe, eventually returning to Paris. Seeing the plight of the poor there inspired him to create what he called a *"bureau des addresses et des recontres,"* an office and job board for the unemployed. Its instant success prompted Renaudot to expand to include goods for sale, goods wanted, and all sorts of public announcements.[5]

Renaudot wanted to distribute the information he was collecting more widely, so he started the newspaper *La Gazette*. After all, why would you limit your distribution to only the people who had the time, ability, and inclination to walk to your job board when you could deliver that information directly to exponentially more viewers with a simple print? He thereby became both the first French journalist and the inventor of the personal ad.[6] Advertising and journalism would be inextricably linked from then on.

While the printing press democratized information almost overnight, transportation hadn't yet evolved into an efficient way to get ideas or products in front of a huge audience. Early newspapers remained hyper-local affairs. And in the early days of the Industrial Revolution in both Europe and the United States, hyper-local news was just fine for average citizens, who weren't yet traveling far from their birthplaces. Consequently, early ads were often placed by individuals rather than by what we would think of as brands or organizations. By the middle of the 17th century, US and European newspapers were inviting readers to place ads for real estate, ships, or goods for sale.[7]

Of course, these early proto-ads weren't recognizable as advertising or marketing in the way we think of them today. They made simple statements of facts without embellishment (or even many adjectives), like this one for coffee:

Very good ground Coffee
for Eight Shillings a Pound, 14 Ounces to the Pound' which is the
Extent of what it makes when properly roasted, to be Sold by Israel
Eaton, living near the Mill Bridge; -- where Persons may have Chocolat
[sic] and also Coffee ground for Eighteen Pence a Pound.[8]

Newspapers were printed daily and covered local news and current events, but many intellectuals wanted to create publications that allowed for deeper, more thoughtful exploration of particular topics. In 1663, German theologian and poet Johann Rist created a periodical called *Erbauliche Monaths-Unterredungen* (*Edifying Monthly Discussions*), which summarized new books and welcomed scholarly articles. The periodical was published for five years and spawned similar journals in England, France, and Italy.[9] The magazine-publishing boom was off and running, with specialized publications appearing throughout Europe and America from the 1660s to the mid-1800s.

But here's the interesting thing about these early magazines: they were expensive and aimed at the intellectual elite. Proto-ads, an integral part of newspapers from their inception, were absent from these highbrow periodicals. This purity seems to have two root causes: advertisers weren't interested in paying to reach niche audiences, and magazine publishers wanted to focus on maintaining their commitment to fostering intelligent discourse free from outside influence. Printing and distribution costs were covered by subscription fees rather than advertising revenue.

By the 1830s, however, once the Industrial Revolution had improved printing technology, the cost of printing and mailing magazines took a sharp downward turn. Publishers began producing less expensive publications aimed at broader audiences and featuring content designed for entertainment rather than edification. In 1893, copies of *McClure's Magazine* began selling for 15 cents each (compared to the 25 or 35 cents most other magazines charged), setting a new price point for the medium.

By some estimates, this drop in price tripled the size of the magazine-buying public.[10] And, now that magazines were reaching a wider readership, advertisers wanted in. By 1900, advertising was fully integrated into the magazine business. For emerging brands, the timing couldn't have been any better.

Meet the Brands

From 1760 to 1840, things got interesting for business owners and entrepreneurs. The Industrial Revolution brought improvements to mass production of the printed word and enabled the manufacture and packaging of consumer goods on a previously unheard-of scale. Before the Industrial Revolution, manufacturers were hamstrung by limitations on both supply and demand and sold their wares in the immediate vicinity only, with little to no competition for customers. Once manufacturers could produce and distribute more widely, however, they began to look for ways to persuade a larger number of people to buy their products.

In his 1984 book *The Complete Guide to Advertising*, Torin Douglas recounts, "Firms such as Cadbury and Fry started packaging their products, not simply to protect them and preserve their quality, but also to *establish* their quality by the use of the company's own name."[11]

This is a vaguely interesting concept in the abstract, but when you learn the stories of the individuals who understood what was happening and moved to exploit it, it's a fascinating scenario that bears close scrutiny for modern marketers, who will be working in times of rapid change for the foreseeable future. This case study is that of Josiah Wedgwood, grandfather of Charles Darwin and a brilliant marketer way back before that was even a thing.

Born in 1730, Wedgwood was, like many people in his family and village, apprenticed to be a potter. While training, he realized two things: he could grow a business far beyond his immediate surroundings and he could choose to create products that were not solely utilitarian. In the mid-18th century, these ideas were revolutionary. Many people ate meals out of week-old-bread bowls; a plate of any kind was a luxury. To produce only the highest-quality ceramics (Josiah was famous for smashing imperfect items with his walking stick) was almost ludicrous.

And that's what Josiah Wedgwood did. He put his name on every piece he made, creating, arguably, the first recognizable brand in the Western world. He also embarked on one of the first, and riskiest, influencer marketing campaigns in the world.

In 1771 Wedgwood spent $2.7 million sending unsolicited samples of his pottery to one thousand wealthy Germans—a gamble that, if it didn't pay off, could have bankrupted him. But it did pay off. More than half of his "influencers" immediately ordered more of his pottery.

Of course, like any Agile marketer, he knew his gamble would probably pay off; he had already proved the validity of this approach with smaller, test versions of this campaign.

Several years *before* the send to one thousand households, he gave Queen Charlotte, the wife of King George III, a breakfast set, which prompted her to order a full tea service a few years later. Not content to simply ship the order and call it a successful experiment, Wedgwood branded the tea service as Queen's Ware and sold copies of it to the public. When he was commissioned to produce bespoke china for Catherine the Great of Russia, Wedgwood again leveraged the power of early influencers by displaying the finished work in his London showrooms for months before shipping it to Russia. The display drew huge crowds and earned him tons of free media coverage.[12]

Brand awareness, influencer marketing, and Agile iterations—all happening nearly three hundred years ago.

Let's not forget that Wedgwood backed all of this hype with impeccable quality merchandise. He trained employees to meet his exacting standards, refused to ship flawed pieces, and constantly refined his manufacturing techniques to be sure that his product lived up to its marketing messages.

Unfortunately, not all who profited from the emergence of brands held themselves to the same ethical principles.

Trust Me, I'm Lying

As the Industrial Revolution chugged on, the consumer goods market became increasingly saturated. As in our current era, marketers were learning on the fly, desperately trying to figure out what they could do to convince the emerging middle class to part with a little of their new-found disposable income. Unfortunately for every marketer since, embellishment or outright lying quickly became the go-to tactic.

Whether it was in a newspaper or on a shelf at newly formed retailers like Wanamaker's and Marshall Field & Company, packaging and advertising copy had to rapidly differentiate one product from another. This led to truly outlandish claims, particularly from the sellers of patent medicines. Their messaging was so extreme that it prompted government intervention in the United States—although not until decades later in 1906. It's worth noting that when the Proprietary Association, a trade association of patent-medicine producers, opposed early attempts at regulation, they were joined wholeheartedly by the newspaper publishers who had come to rely on their advertising revenue.[14] The hand-in-glove partnership between journalism and advertising was still going strong.

Before the passage of the Pure Food and Drug Act in 1906, advertisers ran ads like the following:

For Your Health
Asthma Cigarettes
Since 1882
For the temporary relief of paroxysms of asthma
Effectively treats: asthma, hay fever, foul breath, all diseases of the throat, head colds, canker sours [sic], bronchial irritations
Not recommended for children under 6

While entertaining in retrospect, these ads provided false hope to many sufferers. They also contributed to serious health problems, including dependence on drugs, such as cocaine and alcohol, that many of the products contained. In fact, the above-cited ad for cigarettes is unusual only in its suggestion that it was unsuitable for children.

To better understand how the fledgling profession of advertising contributed to problems with patent-medicine claims, consider a product that owed its success almost entirely the rapid adoption of advertising: Lydia Pinkham's Vegetable Compound.

Lydia Pinkham, unlike the spokespeople for some similar products, was a real woman. She was a Quaker who lived in

Massachusetts and occasionally brewed a remedy for "female complaints" to share with friends. Her sons persuaded her to turn this altruistic hobby into a business in 1875. She mixed a huge batch of the remedy (which contained four kinds of roots, fenugreek seed, and 19 percent alcohol) and bottled it. After failing to drum up sufficient business through a four-page printed pamphlet, her son Will gambled 60 dollars, a substantial sum at the time, on a full-page ad in the *Boston Herald*. The response was instantaneous— three wholesalers immediately rushed in with orders, with more to follow—and the Pinkhams were hooked on advertising. They poured most of their early earnings into more advertising, drawing only modest living expenses for themselves.[15]

For the first decade after product launch, Harlan Page Hubbard, an agent from New Haven, Connecticut, handled all the advertising for the Vegetable Compound. He had no scruples about using language that was, by Victorian standards, graphic to the point of vulgarity. Despite their objections, Hubbard put pressure on publishers to run customer testimonials featuring detailed descriptions of the product's effects and the physical ailments that it cured. With many newspapers accepting cases of Vegetable Compound in lieu of cash payment and selling it to local wholesalers and druggists who would then pass it on to consumers with the help of ads, their objections cannot have been overly loud. Another common incestuous behavior was for newspapers to print favorable editorials about Mrs. Pinkham to garner her favor—and the renewal of her advertising contract.

Everyone made money and got along fine until the Pinkhams discovered that Hubbard's unscrupulous behavior wasn't limited to strong-arming publishers. He was also buying ad space at low rates and selling it to the Pinkhams for as much as 50 percent more, despite assuring them that his markup would never exceed 15 percent.

The Pinkhams, in reaction, slashed their advertising budget and saw annual sales fall from $260,000 to $58,000 until they hired a new agent in 1890 and resumed advertising. Staying this course for ten years, they devoted an average of 44 percent of their revenue to advertising. Sales increased 2,500 percent.

To merchants like the Pinkhams, to advertising agents like Hubbard, and to newspapers that got paid to promote products and services, these arrangements were, if not commendable, at least acceptable. But this early incarnation of the advertising profession was not well-liked. Although they provided a necessary component of early capitalism and a remarkably effective means of selling products, advertisers were not a revered group:

> Advertising was considered an embarrassment—the retarded child, the wastrel relative, the unruly servant kept backstairs and never allowed into the front parlor. A firm risked its credit rating by advertising; banks might take it as a confession of financial weakness. Everyone deplored advertising. Nobody—advertiser, agent, or medium—took responsibility for it...In the absence of government regulation, the entire business was conducted in a half-light of bunkum and veiled appearances.[15]

Fortunately for those of us who enjoy our marketing careers, this stigma would soon begin to fade, thanks to a few early practitioners who spurned misleading language in favor of the heretical practice of telling the truth.

The Straight-Talk Backlash

Like Josiah Wedgwood, who insisted on producing only the highest-quality pottery so that he could market it with confidence, some sellers and advertisers rejected the manipulative language favored by patent medicines. Among them was John E. Powers, whom *Advertising Age* has called "the father of creative advertising."[16] He famously claimed that "fine writing [in ads] is offensive" and insisted on concentrating on facts and steering clear of hyperbole.

Later in his career, Powers was retained by a Pittsburgh clothing company on the verge of bankruptcy. "There is only one way out," he told them, "tell the truth...the only way to salvation lies in large and immediate sales."

The ad that Powers produced read, "We are bankrupt. This announcement will bring our creditors down on our necks. But if you come and buy tomorrow we shall have the money to meet them. If not we will go to the wall." Sympathetic customers answered the call in droves.

The straight-talking, conversational style of Powers and his followers was a distinct and direct counterpoint to the big promises and flowery language made popular by patent-medicine ads. The tell-it-like-it-is tradition continued as more copywriters came onto the scene, while the flowery-language school shifted toward psychological persuasion and away from bald-faced lies.

Theodore F. MacManus was the most vocal and prolific advocate of the emerging practice of advertising "by atmosphere and suggestion," says Stephen Fox in *The Mirror Makers*. "Eye fixed on the future, he scorned quick, spectacular campaigns aimed at fast sales. Instead, in the same unhurried way that two people became friends, he aimed to build a friendship based on a slow accumulation of favorable impressions."[17] MacManus would have been right at home on a modern content marketing team.

By the early twentieth century, when the US government was about to crack down on patent-medicine claims, MacManus was producing copy that "gently wooed potential buyers, convincing them in melting prose that the Cadillac...was an irreproachable luxury purchase."[18] Not only did he go for the wooing, long-term soft sell, MacManus implicitly understood the concept of brand loyalty long before anyone was calling it that. "The real suggestion to convey," he insisted, "is that the man manufacturing the product is an honest man, and that the product is an honest product, *to be preferred above all others.*"[19] Fix our good friend MacManus in your mind, because he inspired many future advertising luminaries, including arguably the most famous adman, David Ogilvy.

Despite these more nuanced tactics, patent-medicine advertising remained a stain on the advertising industry's reputation. Even the passage of the Pure Food and Drug law of 1906 had little impact. Although the law required product labels to list active ingredients, it put no limitations on how the products could be advertised. Manufacturers of patent medicine adjusted their labels to comply with the new rules, adding that they were now "guaranteed" under the Pure Food and Drug law for good measure, and continued advertising in exactly the same way. Their sales rose 60 percent from 1902 to 1912.[20]

Neither did the integrity of the press fare well. When patent medicine sellers contracted to buy newspaper advertising, they included clauses that terminated the ad contract in any state whose legislature passed any bill harmful to the manufacturer's business interests. Some contracts prohibited the newspaper from running any unfriendly editorial matter.[21] For many publications, the loss of patent medicine's revenue would mean bankruptcy, so they traded away their freedom of expression for survival.

It was precisely these types of dealings that put advertising outside the realm of respectability in the early twentieth century. Popular literature took up the subject with gusto, roundly vilifying advertising men (and they were almost universally men at the time) in novels (*The Clarion* by Samuel Hopkins Adams and *H.R.* by Edwin Lefevre), plays (*It Pays to Advertise* by Roi Cooper Megrue), and short stories (the character of Lancelot Todd by Sinclair Lewis published in *Metropolitan* magazine). You probably didn't encounter any of these in your high school English class. That's to be expected, because most of them weren't great works of literature. Yet even "[i]f ephemeral as literature, these works took on historical significance as unanimous condemnations of advertising; no dramatists or writers of fiction yet came forward to praise the trade in their work."[22]

As they became entrenched in the popular consciousness through printed fiction, advertisers themselves had seemingly figured out this whole print thing. Ad men may not have been popular, but they were effective. As the annual volume of advertising doubled between 1918 and 1920, it became increasingly clear that effective advertising could deliver customers and profit to businesses of all types. Having weathered the storm of close association with patent medicine, advertising as a profession began to enjoy a taste of respectability, if not affection, in society:

The advertising man is the enfant terrible of the time, unabashed before the eternities," declared S.N. Behrman in the New Republic in 1919. 'Even war needs him, to say nothing of Swift and Company.' He was typically young, said Behrman, handsome, impeccably dressed, with sleek hair and snappy shoes. His prominence in American life made him as self-satisfied as a movie actor. 'The cornerstone of the most respectable American institutions; the newspapers and magazines depend on him; Literature and Journalism are his hand maidens. He is the Fifth Estate.'[23]

But just as marketers were getting the hang of communicating effectively in the print medium, another channel came along that would throw them for a loop.

This Program Brought to You By...

The reader of a newspaper has an option whether he will read or not, but if a speech by the president is to be used as the meat in a sandwich of two patent-medicine advertisements, there will be no radio left.
Herbert Hoover, 1924[24]

Since the medium came into being, radio, like the newspaper, has enjoyed a mutually beneficial relationship with advertising. (At least that's the case in the US; in the UK the BBC has been consistently ad-free.) As early as 1922, WEAF in New York offered 10-minute advertising slots for $100. But this was an anachronism; sponsored shows like *The Eveready Hour* and *The Goodrich Silver-Masked Tenor* were the primary vehicle for early radio ads and remained so for much of the medium's history.

The most well-known example of this early incarnation of sponsored content is the soap opera, so named because detergent brands often produced the program. But other brands were also major players in the early days of radio, helped along by fledgling advertising agencies that turned their previous print experience to radio and attempted to help clients navigate the emerging channel.

For example, the advertising agency Benton & Bowles was perched on the precipice of bankruptcy during radio's early years. Then they launched a radio variety show for their client Maxwell House. *The Maxwell House Showboat* pushed coffee sales up 85 percent in a year and established Benton & Bowles as masters of the new medium.[25]

This type of story was, and still is, the lure of marketing and advertising: we're all just one big idea away from becoming the next amazing case study. There were success stories aplenty in the 1920s, with advertisers themselves chief among them: "Now fifty years beyond his old associations with snake oil and consumption cures, the adman could regard himself as a regular guy, just another businessman. In popular fiction of the 1920s, the adman often appeared as the hero: the copy cub who at the last minute writes a brilliant ad, snares the client, and gets the promotion and the girl."[26]

While agencies positioned themselves as indispensable cogs in the media and advertising machine, a debate arose: should that machine even exist? Some listeners were apprehensive about advertising worming its way, via radio, into the intimate family circle. But most were pleased to enjoy a wide variety of programming that was "brought to you by" one brand or another. That phrase made it clear that without brand involvement, your favorite show simply wouldn't exist. This attention barter system—the unspoken agreement under which audiences exchanged some of their attention for entertainment and information—drove the relationship between marketers and consumers for decades. Since both parties benefitted— advertisers got the attention they needed to make sales while the audience got a diverting show —the system worked well at its inception.

The attention barter system even survived, largely intact, the advent of the next huge media disruption, television. But this new channel split the audience's attention even further (for entertainment, they could now read, listen to the radio, or watch television), lessening the effectiveness of an ad on any medium and signaling the beginning of the fragmentation frenzy that still grips marketing today.

The Time Advertising Lost Its Way

Audience fragmentation has certainly made marketing a more challenging profession in the twenty-first century, but we also labor under a burden of considerable mistrust. Fair or not, our industry's historical behavior in advertising and marketing has earned us the skepticism with which we're now regarded. We've seen examples of less-than-stellar behavior by some early advertisers—secretly marked-up commissions, unethical relationships with publishers, misleading copy—but we also need to examine how advertising addressed the Great Depression, its first large-scale challenge as a legitimate industry. Advertising's behavior during this most challenging and tumultuous period did little to endear it to the public.

The end of the 1920s witnessed the launch of *Advertising Age*, a trade journal whose name alone tells us a lot about how the advertising industry saw itself at the time. At the same time, popular public figures like Franklin D. Roosevelt and Calvin Coolidge lauded the profession:

> If I were starting life over again, I am inclined to think that I would go into the advertising business in preference to almost any other...It is essentially a form of education; and the progress of civilization depends on education.
>
> Franklin D. Roosevelt[27]

It is the most potent influence in adapting and
changing the habits and modes of life, affecting
what we eat, what we wear, and the work and play
of the whole nation. Advertising ministers to the
spiritual side of trade.

Calvin Coolidge[28]

Then, in October of 1929, it all came crashing down. After the
stock market plummeted, advertisers maintained an optimistic tone
in the ads they produced, but they could *not* maintain their billings.
The annual volume of advertising dropped from $3.4 billion in 1929
to $2.3 billion in 1931, and bottomed out at $1.3 billion in 1933, a
mere 38 percent of the pre-Depression level.[29]

Forced to lay off workers and constantly worried about their
own solvency, clients put considerable pressure on their advertising
agencies. They demanded rebates and special deals. They wanted
ads that were more effective but cost less (which sounds like every
marketing planning meeting, ever). Advertisers did their best, but
nothing worked. They "kept repeating the same old promises and
predicting the return of good times," but things kept getting worse.[30]
They abandoned the flowery language and soft sell popularized by
MacManus; they decided that hard times required a hard sell.

During the Depression, "the advertising agencies adopted fixed
grins and preached optimism...The hard sell got harder; more sex
appeared in advertising. The bitter public glanced disdainfully at ads
for products they could no longer afford. With the glory days of the
1920s at an end, advertising would never again regain its coquettish
charm."[31]

In 1934, Bruce Barton, one of the original founders of BBDO,
lamented, "Under the lash of bad business ideals have been

abandoned, standards have sunk." The waves of "silly advertisements, dishonest advertisements, disgusting advertisements cast discredit upon the business and put us on the defensive."[32] He was right. Americans were less credulous than they had been during the patent-medicine heyday at the turn of the century, and they clamored for government intervention to protect them from the maliciousness of Madison Avenue. "Under a new label, 'consumerism,' a diverse and growing popular movement," public pressure "presented advertising with its most severe emergency since the patent-medicine days."[33]

The government obliged in 1938 with the passage of the Wheeler-Lea amendments to the Federal Trade Commission Act. The amendments declared "deceptive acts of commerce" unlawful. They added injunctive powers to the FTC's cease-and-desist orders that resulted in eighteen injunctions being handed down in the next two years.[34] Things might have gotten far worse for the advertising industry, but the consumerist movement, like everything else, was superseded by the arrival of World War II. As advertisers helped make the conflict palatable to the American public, they regained some of the respectability (if not actual respect) they'd lost during the early days of the Depression.

As the Second World War ended, America started looking for the new normal. The bomb had been dropped, tens of millions had died, and the economy was in overdrive; it was obvious that things would not return to the pre-war status quo. Standing ready to help show Americans exactly how they should be living was an invention that had been quietly incubating for decades: the television.

CHAPTER TWO

You Can Buy Happiness and Other Lies from the TV Age

*"Television is the strongest drug we've ever had to dish out.
Maybe that's why our hands shake a little when we take
the cork out of the bottle, but we'll get over that."*
Leo Burnett to the National Television Council in 1949 [35]

The television era is responsible for a great many changes not only in the marketing profession, but in the way that marketers as a group are perceived. It also represented the first serious clash between an established and an emerging medium, namely radio versus television. Marshall McLuhan, an early observer of television's growing power, remarked, "Our official culture is striving to force the new media to do the work of the old. These are difficult times because we are witnessing a clash of cataclysmic proportions between two great technologies."[36] Since the subsequent history of marketing exists in one cataclysmic clash after another, we would benefit from reviewing TV's early days.

When it first arrived on the landscape of household media, television was an unknown commodity. Marketers and advertisers weren't sure exactly how they should approach it, but they knew that cracking the TV code would provide huge payoffs. Advertisers had long intuited the power of effective imagery (even though they didn't yet know our brains process visual information 60,000 times faster than other types of input), and TV would give them the opportunity to display an enormous number of powerful images to a fairly captive audience.

Nonetheless, advertising on TV started out slow—$12 million in the US in 1949—but grew quickly, to $158 million in 1952.

A dilemma, at least for brands, was that pouring money into creating a brand presence on television didn't eliminate the need to maintain existing radio campaigns. TVs didn't eliminate radios any more than radios had eliminated magazines and newspapers. Brands now had to navigate their way around a three-headed marketing monster, and individuals who could help them do that effectively became practically god-like. The Mad Men who could effectively manipulate buying behavior through ads became a cultural icons thanks, in large part, to television's reach and ubiquity. However, the power of advertising executives didn't come without a cost; popular media increasingly depicted them as immoral, alcohol-sodden rogues whose motives and means were both suspect.

This distrust reached its zenith during the re-energized consumer movement of the 1960s, but even during advertising's first boom in the 1920s consumers were feeling commoditized. Part of the problem was that television and radio exponentially expanded the reach of advertising and marketing messages without doing much to improve their personalization. Since targeting, as we know it, did not exist, "spray and pray" was the only way to manage advertising campaigns.

Large audiences were, of course, what made advertising an efficient means of distributing a message. As we'll see when we observe digital media, advertising gives way to marketing as audiences fragment. But that's getting ahead of the story a bit. First we need to go back much earlier in television's history, when this new medium was considered the ultimate source of reliable information and captivating entertainment. This period was also a brave new world for advertising, which struggled until a handful of smart marketers started using television shows as inspiration for their ads. Once they began mirroring and mimicking the content people had come to see, using the conventions of the medium for their message, things really took off.

If TV Said It, It Must Be True

Even in its earliest, grainiest, least impressive moments, there was no overlooking the power of the boxes appearing in homes around the United States. In 1939, when RCA was preparing to inaugurate its program service, its president, David Sarnoff, predicted:

> With the advent of television, the combined emotional results of both seeing and hearing an event or a performance at the instant of its occurrence become new forces to be reckoned with, and they will be much greater forces than those aroused by audition only. The emotional appeal of pictures to the mass of people is everywhere apparent. [37]

Despite an understanding of this unmatched potential, early incarnations of television news programs were basically radio shows with graphics added. I can't help but compare the rocky nature of the first tentative forays out of radio and into TV to the first corporate attempts at creating websites. Remember when brands simply digitized their existing print brochures, slapped a "www" in front of their name, and deemed themselves cutting-edge? Good times. With television and again with the Internet, we made it up as we went along. With no understanding of how the new medium operated, everyone assumed that it would work pretty much like the old medium, except that it would be a lot cooler.

For years of broadcasting, no news anchors ever announced that they would "go live" to an event happening outside of the studio. News programs relied on newsreel footage, maps, and other still imagery to supplement the commentary of their television personalities. In many cases, the folks who read the news on the radio were simply plopped in front of a camera and told to carry on as usual. One such newscaster, Lowell Thomas, would sometimes refuse to bother coming into the studio, preferring to perform the broadcast from his home. He could still get away with it because there were 100 million radio listeners who didn't know (or care about) his broadcast location, compared to only 2,500 television viewers. When Lowell was a no-show, the TV audience got "the Television Man," Ray Forrest, a far more informal and physically attractive announcer who was part of the early wave of performers to successfully hitch their fortunes to those of the new medium.[40]

As with radio, early television, from drama to variety show, was broadcast live. It wasn't until 1956 that recording multiple takes and editing them together became technologically feasible. Up until that point, whatever you saw on your television had actually happened. Even after retakes became possible, they were rarely used because edits to the videotape on which they were recorded had to be made by hand using a razor blade. Although challenging for multi-camera dramas, the lack of technical sophistication lent other early programming, particularly sports and news broadcasts, an air of authenticity.

While in-the-moment TV programs like soap operas and variety shows wrestled with the logistics of an audience who could see everything they did, news programs were basking in the trust and credibility ushered in by this new medium. In fact, TV really began to take hold in the United States thanks to coverage of the 1948 political conventions in Philadelphia. There was so much interest in what the stations provided that as many as 10 million Americans saw at least some televised convention coverage even though there were only about 300,000 sets in the country at the time. Group viewing in living rooms, department stores, and at special events was beginning to establish TV as a cultural touchstone.[39]

Four years later, during the next election cycle, about 60 million viewers tuned in to watch at least some of the conventions on television. Following this coverage, Jack Gould of the *New York Times* reflected that TV news had now "won its spurs" and become "a welcome addition to the Fourth Estate."[42]

Unfortunately for news programs, the exponential growth in audience size that they had helped create was rendering them obsolete. "In short, as TV expanded its reach, and as the networks, individual stations, and advertisers developed programs that were most likely to attract large numbers of viewers and make their investments pay off, news personnel came to recognize that they would occupy no more than a small niche on network schedules. Holding on to that niche would depend on their ability to make their programming compatible with the entertainment shows and advertising that had become the medium's staples."[41]

Big Audience, Small Oligopoly

From a marketing perspective, this historical moment in the mid-1950s is where things started to break down. The size of the television audience was skyrocketing. The technology was finally catching up with demand, lowering TV prices and allowing everybody to get a set (or three). Advertisers could now reach millions of people with a single television ad, and if they coordinated that with some print and radio spend, they were essentially blanketing their target audience. Consumers had little choice but to sit and, well, consume the ads, because their viewing options were limited. In fact, until the widespread distribution of cable television, you could count your programming choices on your fingers.

The balance that had sustained the attention barter system had swung too far toward advertisers.

Before television reached market saturation, advertisers had to consider the people they hoped to reach when designing campaigns. Since "anyone with a few dollars and some back issues of *Popular Science* could put a radio station on the air,"[43] there was considerable competition for listeners' ears and attention. If one station's advertising got too intrusive, improper, or uninteresting, a quick twist of the dial brought listeners to one of that station's competitors. Alternatively (and displaying behavior unthinkable to a television viewer), radio listeners displeased with the content would simply turn off the radio and walk away.

Television audiences, on the other hand, were spellbound, unable to tear themselves from the magic of the flickering screen. Even the earliest adopters, those who braved the high prices, lackluster programming, and unreliable technology, became addicts:

The select few [who purchased television sets]
almost overnight altered their eating and sleeping
schedules to accommodate viewing hours. Evening
hours previously reserved for family conversation
were now devoted to the set, which required two
senses instead of radio's one. It also demanded quiet
attention—except when conversation concerned
what was on the screen.[44]

Once the lure of the boob tube became inescapable, advertisers
knew they had actual captive audiences. Nobody would even think of
turning off an episode of "I Love Lucy" because there was a mildly
annoying commercial in the middle. But while the programming
was becoming more enticing and the audience larger, the mechanics
that had underpinned the television industry since its inception were
actively preventing the introduction of more programming choices
for viewers.

Led by the forward-thinking pioneer David Sarnoff, who had
been championing the idea of television for decades, RCA opened its
regular television service on April 30, 1939, with a telecast from the
New York World's Fair. In his speech, Sarnoff waxed poetic, despite
his general insensibility to the programming side of television (he
was a hardware geek at heart): "Now we add radio sight to sound.
It is with a feeling of humbleness that I come to this moment of
announcing the birth in this country of a new art so important in
its implications that it is bound to affect all society. It is an art which
shines like a torch of hope in a troubled world. It is a creative force
which we must learn to utilize for the benefit of all mankind."

Sarnoff's words, like practically everything he did, were calculated.
In 1939 all television stations operated under an experimental status,

which meant the Federal Communication Commission (FCC) had not granted them a commercial license. That, in turn, meant they could not sell advertising around their programs.

RCA saw the potential profit just around the bend, so they were willing to run stations at a loss while lobbying furiously for the FCC to acknowledge television's parity with radio and grant commercial licenses. Its technological advantages gave RCA a massive head start in the race to manufacture satisfactory television sets, and two of its major competitors, Zenith and Philco, worked diligently to convince the FCC and the public that commercial TV was not ready for licensing.[45]

Although they met with initial success, Sarnoff's decision in 1938 to go ahead and market receivers without FCC approval forced other manufacturers to reach an agreement with RCA about broadcast standards, which represented the final hurdle in gaining FCC approval for commercial television. These standards were necessary to ensure that every licensed TV station would transmit the same number of picture lines, allowing all sets manufactured in the United States to receive every broadcast TV signal. When the agreement came through in 1941, the FCC quickly announced it would begin to grant commercial TV licenses. The first went to W2XBS in New York City (now known as WNBT), which gained its license on July 1, 1941.

A scant three years later, television studios were dark. The start of World War II put production almost completely on hold and radio maintained supremacy while the attention of the world was directed to more pressing matters. As the conflict began to wind down, RCA and rival DuMont prepared to fire up their manufacturing plants to take advantage of years of pent-up spending urges in the American populace.

CBS and Zenith, who were far less prepared, threw a wrench into television's restart to buy themselves time to catch up. Their play was to convince the FCC to delay further legitimization of black-and-white broadcasting in favor of the color system that CBS had been developing. This was the real issue at the heart of the FCC battle, but the placeholder was a debate over something far less glamorous: the area on the broadcast spectrum that would be used for television broadcasting. CBS's fledgling system required UHF frequencies, but before the war TV broadcasting had been at VHF. This status quo benefitted RCA, whose manufacturing facilities were poised to churn out thousands of sets tuned to the VHF frequencies.

In 1945, the FCC ruled that, with some adjustment, television would continue to be broadcast along pre-war channels. It was a victory for RCA and a setback for consumers (and the marketers who would try to reach them), because the VHF band made fewer channels available, reducing the options and the level of competition between stations. The oligopoly that resulted would remain in place for decades until UHF returned to the fray and cable television became widely available in the 1980s.[46]

This lopsided situation meant that, almost from its inception, the reach and personalization of TV evolved at vastly different rates. It was a disconnect that, incidentally, has also plagued the Internet and digital media until very recently. Marketers and advertisers could reach enormous audiences, but they could only reach them en masse. Gathering huge swaths of the audience in one place was the only way to justify the rapidly swelling costs of producing ads for television, but it was also setting up the rejection of mass media in general, and television in particular, that is bedeviling marketers and advertisers today.

But once again, I'm jumping ahead of the story—it moves so fast! Before things got harder for our predecessors on Madison Avenue, they got a whole lot easier.

It's the Best of Times. Now Go Buy Something.

"Regardless of our current interpretation of the 1950s, however, one cannot overlook the conformity that infused the era's advertising. Leafing through magazines from the decade reveals a striking focus on glamour, novelty, sparkle, and exhilaration. It seems as if advertising served as a kind of mass lobotomy, ramming these ideas into consumers as a way of inculcating the positive messages coming out of a postwar, happy, healthy United States."
Keith Booker and Bob Batchelor, *Mad Men: A Cultural History*[47]

The gleam of the 1950s has been tarnished by the passage of time; it certainly wasn't nonstop suburban bliss for everyone, particularly women, racial minorities, and anyone whose sexual preference wasn't strictly heterosexual. But for the advertising industry, there wasn't much of a downside.

In the 1920s, advertising enjoyed its first moments of ascendancy by acting as the handmaiden to the burgeoning culture of American capitalism. Since that time, it had helped persuade Americans to heed the call of patriotism during the First and Second World Wars, and helped oversee the resurgence of the American economy following the victories in Europe and Asia. Aided enormously by the power of television, consumerism took hold of the American consciousness and held on tight, maintaining a vice-like grip that lasted into the 50s.

Fueled by the twin explosions of automobile manufacturing, which produced expensive consumer goods with minimal variation from one to the next, and television viewing, gross advertising went up 75 percent during the 1950s, rising faster than the GNP, personal income, or any other economic index.[48] But underneath this raw data lurked a growing discrepancy between the need to turn a profit and the drive to produce genuinely interesting ads.

In the introduction to their collection, *Mad Men: A Cultural History*, M. Keith Booker and Bob Batchelor argue that initially this potent combination of reach and receptiveness acted like catnip for advertisers, who capitalized on it "by making advertising into a genuine art form; television commercials soon became as well-crafted and as entertaining as many of the programs, thus developing an independent following of their own."[49]

Stephen Fox points out that the sources of these extraordinary pieces were not, however, established agencies like JWT and BBDO, but rather upstarts that had been founded to balance (or reject outright) the old guard's growing reliance on research and predictability.

Many of the most memorable ads of the decade came from Doyle Dane Bernbach (DDB), the first "creative agency" and the source and center of much of advertising's creative revolution. It stormed onto the scene in 1949, delivering powerful campaigns for Ohrbach's department store, Levy's Bakery, Polaroid, and Avis rental cars before producing two of the most iconic ads of all time as part of the first American campaign for Volkswagen. With starkly simple headlines ("Think small." and "Lemon") and photographs that were largely untouched, the DDB ads not only introduced a German car to the American public a scant 15 years after the end of World War II, they created a disturbance in advertising best practices that is still felt today. In 1999, Advertising Age's *The Century of Advertising* named the series the number one campaign of all time.

For Fox, these enduring ads "seemed especially good because they had so little competition." The old guard of agencies produced work that was "safe and dull, without flair or distinction" and as a result, despite enjoying a period of unprecedented prestige and prosperity, "the industry underwent a round of self-flagellation," deploring a lack of creativity among both practitioners and products.[50] This situation was unsurprising given that traditional advertising research focused on quantifying the returns of long-running campaigns, giving it a conservative bias that favored copying ads that had previously been successful. Motivation Research (MR) began to emerge as an effort to discern how an ad would perform prior to its release, but 1950s ad campaigns were more often guided by the philosophy of one of its most dominant personalities, Rosser Reeves.

Reeves coined the term "Unique Selling Proposition (USP)," and argued that once identified, advertising need only repeat the USP until a purchase was practically inevitable. The "Unique" part of the equation, however, was up for interpretation. According to Reeves, there was no need for the USP to be something that only the advertised product possessed; it had merely to be something that *appeared* distinctive.

His willingness to split hairs, combined with his commitment to relentlessly bombarding consumers with his ads, made Reeves the poster boy for all that the public—and advertising practitioners themselves—saw wrong with advertising:

- "I never tried to make *interesting* commercials. Once you've found a Unique Selling Proposition, any good copywriter can write a good ad. The rest is just wordsmithing." Rosser Reeves

- "Too many people are imitating too many other people. Too many advertisers are refusing to explore new paths. Too many advertisers are 'adapting' instead of 'creating'." *Ad Age*, 1952

- "There is very definitely a shortage of really creative people in advertising, and I think about the problem a lot. The account management side of the business is generally regarded today as the most glamorous side." Fairfax Cone, 1954

- "Whether you are talking products, advertising ideas, layout treatments, package design or what have you, we are in the greatest era of monkey-see, monkey-do the world has ever known." Sigurd Larmon, 1956

- "The creative man has lost the chip on his shoulder, the fire in his eye. Success has made him courteous, obedient, cautious. Thin tie, thin skin. He has moved to the suburbs, bought a boat, which he is careful not to rock." Whit Hobbs, BBDO, 1959[51]

The rigorous and repeated application of the ad playbook did not endear advertising to the general public either. For example:

- In 1946, 41 percent of the American people found half or more of all advertising misleading, and 54 percent said it played too much on the audience's emotions.

- In 1950, 80 percent complained that it led people to buy things they didn't need or couldn't afford, and 81 percent called for stricter government regulation.

- In 1952, 68 percent rejected testimonials as insincere.[52]

- Even advertising professionals were ambivalent about their chosen profession. In 1958, a poll of 1,100 advertising people found 85 percent saying they would, if given a second chance, take up the same calling. Eight percent said they would recommend it to their children.[53]

Part of what drove advertising agencies to toe the line and stick with what they knew would work was a paradoxical decline in their profit margins. Although the sheer volume of advertising was increasing to meet the demands of a growing consumer audience, the cost of reaching this audience rose as well. Campaigns now required coordination among a wider variety of agency departments, including not only the creative work of copywriters and artists and the diplomacy of the account executive, but also merchandising, traffic, and media departments.

Merchandising Department: This group worked for clients and for the agency itself. For clients, this department provided advice on product development, including recommending changes to packaging, distribution, pricing, and sales presentations. For their agencies, it tutored creatives on the best selling points for a product, suggested media based on the potential market for a product, and, for account executives, offered insight into a client's selling operations.

Traffic Department: These harried individuals were a bit like project managers, except that they managed individual ads rather than projects. The traffic department shepherded ads through the production process, making schedules and enforcing deadlines to keep the process moving forward.

Media Department: With the increased complexity of the media landscape, these departments were crucial in providing strategies for where ads should appear. They estimated costs, reserved and ordered ad space in publications, paid for placements, and ensured the ads were run correctly.

This complex corporate machinery required lots of cogs, all of whom, in turn, required salaries, expense accounts, benefits, offices, and more. Larger firms even offered public-relations services; Young & Rubicam, McCann-Erickson, Compton, and Benton & Bowles all had PR subsidiaries by 1960. Higher costs meant lower profit margins (with commissions holding at 15 percent), which led to even less risky behavior. It also meant that the "go it alone" trend of the 1920s, which saw new agencies forming each year as young go-getters branched out on their own, was replaced with a multitude of mergers. With clients demanding an ever-increasing range of services from their agencies, the tiny, ultra-creative shop simply wasn't viable.[54]

It was an untenable situation, and by the dawn of the 60s, a creative revolution was underway that would change agency life once again, and, along with it, the public's perception of advertising and its place in the world.

Enter Don Draper, Stage Left

As we've seen, the overworked Mad Man constantly walking the line between sobriety and intoxication isn't the first pop-culture incarnation of advertising practitioners. But thanks to the popular AMC series *Mad Men* (2007-2015), it's easily the best-known to modern audiences. The world of advertising in the 1960s is an ideal subject for fiction of just about any kind, and the immense impact of television on people's daily lives made its popularity on TV in the twenty-first century fitting. For our purposes, *Mad Men* and Mad Men are equally fascinating.

The fictional *Mad Men* reveals how this tumultuous and powerful period in the history of marketing is perceived by our modern popular culture. This perception is, necessarily, colored by our current relationship with ads and marketing. Investigating the show can tell us quite a lot about what it means to work in marketing in 2017.

The historical Mad Men (and, of course, Mad Women) were part of a revolution in the advertising profession that altered the way ads were created and changed the way that many creative advertising professionals thought about their work. During the 60s, people began to see work in advertising as a way to be an artist *and* make enough money to buy food, a perception that persists today.

Mark Tungate recounts in *Adland* that, "the French creative director Olivier Altmann, of the agency Publicis Conseil, once told me, 'Working in advertising is one of the few ways you can be creative and make money at the same time.'"[55]

The creative and cultural revolutions of the 1960s were deeply empowering for writers and graphic artists, and food, clothing, and shelter are nice too. For those who wanted or needed to work, a career on Madison Avenue brought security without the need to sacrifice liberal ideals entirely.

Booker and Batchelor put it this way: "As progressive ideas about ending the war in Southeast Asia and stopping racism at home spread to encompass anti-corporation and anti-big-business tenets, advertising agencies were viewed as a place where young people could work without completely 'selling out' to 'the man.'"[56] While this is only one of many seismic shifts to occur in advertising during the 1960s, it's the one we're going to focus on here because it has the largest influence on how modern marketers see themselves and their work. In addition, the advertising legends of this era, from Mary Wells Lawrence to David Ogilvy and beyond, are referenced in marketing and advertising work today. This period marks one of the earliest points of references for our history-challenged profession.

Finally, by taking a look at how advertisers (who also act as stand-ins for marketers in this historical moment) behave on screen, we can gain a better understanding of what consumers have come to expect from us and the work we produce. As Robert Cluley puts it in *The European Journal of Marketing*, "if we want to rectify marketing's image problem, we cannot hope to do so by redefining marketing—the equivalent of creating a consistent brand identity. Instead, we need to understand marketing's reputation and how it relates to the images of marketing. In this regard, returning to brand theory and practice, we should suspect that the presentation of marketing within mass media texts contributes significantly to marketing's reputation."[57]

In making this argument, Cluley draws heavily on cultivation theory, which bears a brief explanation before we embark on our journey into the 60s. Developed by George Gerbner and Larry Gross in 1976, cultivation theory suggests that continued exposure to television influences, or "cultivates," viewers' perceptions of reality. Gerbner and Gross theorized that the more time people spend consuming media texts, the more likely they are to believe that reality matches its media-created counterparts. They observed this happening with such regularity that "more recent studies do away with surveys of viewers and simply assume that any differences in the portrayal of the social world on television will produce cultivation differentials among viewers."[58]

With that in mind, we can indulge in a brief, close reading of advertising through Matthew Weiner's *Mad Men*-colored glasses.

Advertising Hits a Saturation Point

Booker and Batchelor argue convincingly that the convergence of three areas of American life made advertising a central and inescapable part of US culture in the 1960s:

1. **The general population got smarter, more educated, and more creative.** Improvements in nationwide travel, including rail and air, enabled that creativity to spread rapidly on a scale not previously possible. It became clear that "average" advertising from the 1950s would not work on this more educated and sophisticated audience.

2. **Television and technology helped kill gullibility and cultivate sophistication.** Both advertising clients and consumers "yearned for more sophisticated ads, at least in theory, which caused production and creative costs to increase."

3. **Advertising solidified its place in the blossoming American consumer culture.** While it could be regulated by the government to some extent, advertising was now so tightly integrated into capitalism that it could not be seriously impeded.[59]

While all of these historical factors coalesced, the individuals who excelled at the business of advertising were having a larger-than-usual effect on the industry. As Stephen Fox points out, "The story of advertising in the 1960s was, more than ever, the story of its people: and the people did change. In the previous decade, someone like Rosser Reeves might create ads that bore no resemblance to his own personality. Now, in the sixties, gray-flannel anonymity gave way to personal expression."[60]

William Bernbach, one of the preeminent Mad Men of the era, remarked that, "before us ad people still secretly yearned to be novelists and artists. But we wanted to be part of that whole sixties revolution in music, fashion, and design—and we felt we could do that through advertising."[61] He was right. By being connected to popular culture, the best advertisers of the 1960s turned products into "beautiful little gifts that consumers wanted (or perhaps demanded) to open."[62]

This newfound sensitivity to the external environment helped advertising get a little bit closer to the consumers it had been courting for decades, even if their long-time image problems persisted. In 1969, H.B. Shaffer published a study in CQ Researcher titled "Advertising in a Consumer Society." He concluded that while "most Americans are comfortably attuned to the ubiquitous presence of advertising in their daily lives, they tend to be cynical about its operations."

A similar tension exists in the character of Don Draper, the central figure of *Mad Men*. He's a brilliantly creative advertising professional who clearly enjoys the challenge of coming up with innovative campaign ideas. But his appreciation seems to be more for the deadline-driven thrill of his trade—will he and his team be able to catch the elusive great idea before time runs out and the client walks through the door? Ultimately Don's job doesn't fulfill him on an emotional or spiritual level, creating a void that drives him to neglect his professional responsibilities, get drunk at the office, and make other appallingly bad choices.

You may know modern colleagues who live with this same uneasiness. Compelling the soul of an artist to perform on cue in a pitch meeting can produce magic, as it does in the *Mad Men* episode, "The Wheel," during which Don tells a beautiful story of family life, and how it will sell a new Kodak product. This method can also implode spectacularly, as happens in a later episode when Don reveals that the story at the heart of his new pitch for Hershey actually happened in a whorehouse. But it's this very dichotomy that made advertising and its practitioners such compelling subject matter. That balance, combined with the fact that "we see the outcomes of 1960s-style advertising multiplied geometrically" in our own lives, helped propel *Mad Men* to its critical and popular success.[63]

Concerns about advertising's role in shaping and defining culture are still very much alive. Shaffer's 1969 "summary of the challenges at the heart of the ad game continued to plague the industry into the contemporary era. Strains of this argument are revealed as today's advertising insiders and critics challenge the ubiquity of Google- or Facebook-sponsored ads that employ advanced algorithms to essentially spy on the user and feed her commercial content based on information that most people would consider private."[64]

Ultimately, the cultural and historical situations that formed the background (and often the foreground) of *Mad Men* still impact the professions of marketing and advertising. Whether it's viewers' tension at enjoying clever ads while loathing bothersome pop-ups, or marketers' uneasiness with exploiting their creativity for the profit of corporations, we have by no means worked through the issues that began revealing themselves in 1960s America. Compounding that difficulty is that, while advertisers and audiences were struggling to come to terms with one another, technology was marching toward massive disruptions of its own. Television, which for decades had formed the heart and hub of the relationship between advertisers and audiences, was about to experience cataclysmic changes that would forever alter how advertising worked.

Advertising and Marketing at the
End of the Twentieth Century

After the creative revolution heralded by DDB had trickled down and permeated the industry as a whole, things proceeded rather normally for a couple of decades. There was a return to the 1950s-style reliance on data in the 70s, as agencies reacted to the excesses of the 60s by seeking out "marketing MBAs, people who understood the nuts and bolts of pricing, distribution, and packaging. Instead of rubbing their muses, artists and copywriters were handed the selling idea, with suggestions on how to present it."[65]

Then the winds of change picked up again.

Throughout the 80s, cable television, VCRs, and remote controls became common in upper-middle class families, the magazine industry splintered into more niche publications, and suburban newspapers began to siphon off readership from metropolitan dailies. Much to the chagrin of agencies and brands, the "mass audiences that had made advertising efficient began to fragment."[66]

The most distressing of these trends, at least from the perspective of ad agencies and their clients, was the changes in TV viewing habits. Commercials were expensive to produce and place, which made them major revenue generators for agencies. If consumers could no longer be relied upon to devote short spans of their attention to commercials in exchange for television entertainment, the attention barter system and agency billings were both in serious jeopardy. By the 1980s, it seemed that TV audiences were all too ready to opt out of this decades-long dance.

Stephen Fox identifies three new components of American's viewing habits that emerged in the 80s: "zapping (changing the station w/o getting up from one's comfortable viewing position, to avoid commercials), zipping (fast-forwarding through commercials while watching a program home-recorded on videotape), and grazing, or channel-surfing (flipping restlessly by remote control through scores of programs offered on cable, never tarrying for long, instead of being tied down to the slim, limited pickings of broadcast TV). All these habits meant less predictable impact for TV spots and major headaches for Madison Avenue."[67]

If the relationship between advertisers and consumer prior to the 1980s was like a one-sided conversation, it was pretty clear that, given the opportunity to do so, consumers would walk away. In response, advertisers simply started talking louder and faster. As the arrival of the Internet drew nearer, ads became increasingly ubiquitous. By 1989, the average consumer was exposed to about 7,000 ad messages per day, covering everything from TV commercials to buses.

While ads were proliferating madly, the agencies producing them were consolidating. Mergers and acquisitions abounded as agencies combined in an attempt to deal with rising client demands, increasing needs for a global presence, and a media landscape that just wouldn't sit still. By the early twenty-first century, most people who worked in advertising were employed by one of six major organizations, all of which were in for a wild ride. The fragmentation and disruption they experienced in 80s and 90s was nothing compared to what was coming next.

Audience Fragmentation on Steroids: Cord Cutting and Online Video

As we've seen, the relationship between advertising and television has been one of symbiotic coexistence since the FCC first issued commercial licenses in 1941. Since then, profit has been the primary, and arguably the exclusive, goal of the oligopoly of television producers. Simply put, producers want to make programming that advertisers believe will draw in the highest-value audience. "Highest value" has often meant "largest possible," which has meant appealing to majority opinion, shying away from controversy, and creating images reflective of prevailing cultural norms. As the past 75 years demonstrates, "[a]s long as the same *commercial* system produces television, programming will be designed to suit advertisers."[68]

This "we scratch your back, you scratch ours" arrangement worked out well during the 40s and early 50s, as long as television stations and advertisers had a completely captive audience. The arrangement was simple: the price of entertainment was attention to advertising, and viewers acquiesced because they had no choice. But technology was coming that would improve the watching experience and, eventually, end the attention barter system.

The first major disruption occurred in the 1950s when the remote control arrived to redefine the relationship between television and its audience. As early as 1955, we find newspaper articles celebrating viewers' new power to avoid ads with the help of their remotes, either by muting the sound or changing the channel.[69] Pandora's box was open; once audiences tasted control of their media experience, it quickly became an addiction they would follow from one technology to the next. Advertisers and television producers, meanwhile, dropped into a recurring pattern: head off disruption through litigation and regulation for as long as possible and attempt to harness a new technology themselves only as a last resort.

The next disruption came in the 1980s and took the form of the VCR (videocassette recorder). In our age of on-demand video, it's fun to recall the furor this now-obsolete device caused in the media industry. Movie sales, rentals, and online streaming after the initial theater run now make up a significant percentage of a film's total profits, making them an integral part of its marketing and long-term success.

But in 1984, Universal City Studios did its best to stop Sony from selling VCRs, arguing that the device facilitated copyright violations. The US Supreme Court rejected the argument, ruling that manufacturers of such technology are "not liable for creating a technology that some customers may use for copyright infringing purposes."[70] While it was a film studio that originally brought the lawsuit, the VCR was also a nightmare from advertisers' perspective. In addition to muting ads or changing the channel during commercials, viewers could now skip them entirely on a recorded program without interrupting their media consumption. The captive audience may not have completely broken their chains, but they were on their way.

Two Case Studies in Advertising's Influence

From an advertising and marketing perspective, the Internet still represents an uncharted wilderness. As we'll see, marketers were utterly unprepared for its arrival; we were still navigating previous upheavals in mass media consumption when this entirely new medium exploded onto the scene.

To illustrate just how far the pendulum has swung in the past forty years, I close this chapter by offering two examples of how dramatically technology has changed the relationship between television producers and advertisers. First, a story from the earliest days of commercial television broadcasting illustrates a time when advertisers exercised near-complete dominance over programming. Then we'll travel to the modern era, when even mainstream media companies collude with the audience to avoid the advertising that has come to be seen as a source of irritation that interferes with preferred methods of television consumption.

As we saw in Chapter One, early television advertisers bankrolled the budding industry by sponsoring entire shows rather than buying a 30-second slot somewhere in the middle of an episode. While this relationship led to higher-quality commercials that were shown less frequently, it also put an outsized amount of power in the hands of a show's sponsor. They could cancel a program at any time for any reason, leaving a network scrambling to fill an empty hole in their lineup.

This stranglehold on show content produced some remarkable interventions by advertisers. These included:

- Westinghouse, a maker of light bulbs, initially refused to allow "Studio One" to broadcast their adaption of Rudyard Kipling's "The Light That Failed," believing it would reflect badly on their product.

- Chevrolet refused to allow a pioneer character on a show that it sponsored to "ford" a river.

- Ford nixed a shot of the New York skyline on one of its sponsored shows because the Chrysler building appeared.

- Chrysler cut a mention of Abraham Lincoln's name from a CBS show about the Civil War.

- Mars Candy Company objected to a script that depicted a little girl buying ice cream and cookies rather than candy.

- Camel cigarettes, sponsor of the "Camel News Caravan" and competitor of Lucky Strikes, insisted that during an interview with mobster "Lucky" Luciano, only his real name, "Charles," was to be used.

In 1950, Admiral, a maker of television sets, dropped their sponsored program "The Admiral Broadway Review," not because of any violation of their wishes, but because it was *too* successful. The company was selling so many TVs that it had to stop advertising while it reinvested in capital improvements. Incidentally, this cancellation resulted in NBC pioneering the "magazine plan" advocated by their programming chief Pat Weaver.[71] Rather than offer one advertiser sponsorship for an entire program, Weaver began selling specific slots within a program to different advertisers. The new plan liberated television stations from their dependence on advertisers, but it also created far more commercial breaks in programming. For better or worse, this alternative arrangement ushered in television advertising as we know it today.

As ads got shorter and more of them were crammed into each commercial break, viewers hit their limit. The arrival of the VCR meant they could fast-forward through unwanted interruptions, but, as those of us who once tried to do this will remember, fast forwarding was far more of an art than a science. With the arrival of DVRs (digital video recorders) in 1999 things got more precise, with many remote controls eventually including a button that would advance a recording in convenient, commercial-sized 30-second intervals. Then, in 2012, Dish Network introduced a feature called AutoHop, which would automatically skip ads without consumers having to mash a button repeatedly.

Although universally praised by tech publications, this aggressive move to give customers a more ideal viewing experience at the expense of content providers is a far cry from the intense advertiser interventions of the previous century.

Predictably, ABC, CBS, and Fox Broadcasting Company filed lawsuits against Dish, claiming AutoHop and other Dish features violated their copyrights as well as carriage contracts. By February

2016, all three lawsuits were settled. New carriage agreements with these major networks now include an embargo on the AutoHop feature that ranges from 72 hours to seven days after a show's original airdate.

Such a conflict showcases the rapid and extreme evolution of the relationship between television's major content creators, advertisers, consumers, and media companies like Dish. As audience attention has fragmented again and again, power has shifted into the hands of the consumer and away from studios and advertisers. We have so many options for content consumption that this duo, once all-powerful in the world of television, must now cater to our preferences or be skipped into irrelevance.

PART TWO

Congratulations!
You're a Marketer!

"The advertising industry is in danger of looking like a fat kid playing tag with a group of nimbler opponents who remain tantalizingly out of reach. It will end up red-faced, exhausted, and undignified."
Mark Tungate, *Adland: A Global History of Advertising*[1]

The fundamentals of marketing haven't altered much since the 1890s when Claude Hopkins reminded us that, "advertisers must take the world as we find it. Our business is to win people, not make them over." It's still the job of marketing to meet people where they are with a great product. What *has* changed is the pace. The speed with which new channels appear, gain adoption, and fade away is astonishing—I'm looking at you, Periscope—while, on the whole, marketers remain slow on the uptake. Despite our connections to creative practices, we are a conservative profession, but the plodding pace of yesteryear won't cut it in the digital age: "It took thirty-eight years before 50 million people gained access to radios. It took television thirteen years to earn an audience that size. It took Instagram a year and half."[2]

As channels and media proliferate, the number of audiences is exploding too. As the power of publishing extends further into the population, each person gains the ability to be heard by an audience, however small, that cares about what he or she has to say. Say I reach only 250 people with my weekly blog posts. Whether they're committed consumers, activists, or haters, it's likely I'll impact their actions if my blog provides consistent value and targeted information. Mass messaging rarely works today; it's all about personalized, relevant communication based on niche interests.

Part Two of this book focuses on the recent past and the challenges marketing faces. We look at the second publishing boom, which gives consumers the power to promote or destroy brands in unprecedented ways. Chris Anderson's theory of The Long Tail provides a foundation for us to better understand niche audiences and their communication preferences. We continue the introspective examination of the marketing profession that we started with our close reading of *Mad Men*. The marketer's rocky relationship with the C-suite deserves a look as well; our understanding of history takes us only so far if the CEO's lack of trust limits our impact. And, finally, the plight of the marketers at work: from absurd amounts of overtime to constant interdepartmental conflict, marketers have it pretty rough.

We can't stop the scattering of our audiences, nor can we predict the course of media consumption—social, traditional, digital, or whatever comes next. What we *can* do, once we've gained perspective on where we are and how we got here, is change our approach.

Hear the words of the ever-salty Gary Vaynerchuk from 2013:

> Forget *Mad Men*, and fuck Don Draper. He lived in an easy world where nothing changed for thirty years, where you could spend your whole career working to figure out how the print and television markets worked. This world, the one you and I live in, evolves every second, every day. The skill sets it takes to be a successful entrepreneur, a successful marketer, or a relevant celebrity today is a different skill set than you needed ten years ago, even though that was the skill set that mattered for decades.
>
> I have bad news: Marketing is hard, and it keeps getting harder. But there's no time to mourn the past or to feel sorry for ourselves, and there's no point in self-pity anyway. It is our job as modern-day storytellers to adjust to the realities of the marketplace, because it sure as hell isn't going to slow down for us.[4]

CHAPTER THREE

The Hyper-Fragmentation of Modern Audiences and Their Influences

"It used to be so easy. With the right amount of budget and the right Madison Avenue 'Mad Men,' any business could reach their target audience. But now, the consumer marketplace is fragmented almost beyond recognition." Michael Brenner

When we last left our marketers, they were busily ruining everything on television, radio, and in print.

A book about marketing issues must, of course, consider the digital age. The problems marketers have faced in the last decade originate primarily from two sources:

1. **The proliferation of personal computing power and Internet availability**. As soon as everyone can easily produce quality digital content and reach comparable to what marketers have always provided, the age-old barter of attention for entertainment is well and truly destroyed.

2. **The rapid and unchecked growth of content-distribution channels**. Beginning with email, chat, and

forums and moving rapidly into search, social media, and streaming, the number of places our audiences can go for information, entertainment, and interaction continues to grow. If we hope to maintain a connection with our audiences, we need to be waiting for them wherever they go.

Although widely varied in their real-world incarnations, the trends we wrestle with (and will continue to face in the foreseeable future) can be described in one word: fragmented. If we already considered audiences in the 1990s to be fragmented—they could, after all, watch hundreds of television channels, listen to the radio, or read a magazine or newspaper—then we're now dealing with hyper-fragmentation.

Gutenberg 2.0: Everyone is a Publisher

An obvious contributor to hyper-fragmentation is universal access to the means of publishing. You can now produce just about anything on your laptop, and your content might well be qualitatively indistinguishable from that produced by publishing houses and recording studios.

Writing, in the form of blog posts, books, poetry, social media updates, and more, has never flowed so freely. Over two million blog posts are produced *every day*, and Amazon now has more than four million e-books in its Kindle store, up from 600,000 in 2010.[5]

On the music front, album releases rose from 44,000 in 2004 to 60,000 in 2005, peaking at 106,000 in 2008 before slowing to 75,000 in 2010. Sophisticated video-editing software and high-quality camcorders make independent film production feasible, and potentially lucrative, for anyone.

Podcasts make trivially easy what early HAM radio operators could only dream of doing: democratize the elements of traditional radio broadcasting. With a microphone and an Internet connection, and without FCC limitation or restriction, anyone can reach countless listeners. The Pew Research Center reported in 2016 that 21 percent of Americans over the age of 12 had listened to a podcast in the previous month; that's a 75 percent increase in three years.[6]

To marketers, the democratization of publishing power means that we no longer control what gets said about our brands and products, who hears it, or in what context the message appears.

In their 2007 book *Citizen Marketers*, Ben McConnell and Jackie Huba argue that "A lone person today has a greater chance to create widespread excitement or disrupt a company's reputation without the assistance of the big megaphones of traditional media."[7] They illustrate their point with the story of George Masters, a vocational-school teacher and aspiring digital animator who honed his craft by creating an animated video of a dancing iPod. Masters called the 60-second animation "Tiny Machine," uploaded it to his website, and then asked a few Mac fan sites for feedback. He had no affiliation with Apple Computer other than being a long-time customer and fan, but as McConnell and Huba put it, "a casual observer might not have been faulted for seeing 'Tiny Machine' as the work of a hot creative director inventing a new, albeit retro, iPod branding schema for Apple."[8]

"Tiny Machine" took the Internet by storm, garnering praise from Apple fan sites before being picked up by advertising and marketing bloggers. Newspapers and magazines jumped on the story, featuring the ad and its creator in stories and interviews. A month after he uploaded it, Masters' "ad" had been viewed more than 500,000 times. It eventually landed him a job with a California production company.

What's on the flipside? Negative online reviews, scathing blog posts, tweets, and Facebook posts can do immeasurable damage to seemingly robust brands. In March of 2008, the band Sons of Maxwell took a United Airlines flight from Halifax to Nebraska. They checked a $3,500 guitar, which was labeled "fragile." During a stop in Chicago someone in the seat behind them pointed out the baggage handlers outside the window, who were tossing the guitars around haphazardly. The band's lead singer, Dave Carroll, looked up, horrified to see his 710 Taylor guitar "being heaved without regard by the United baggage handlers."[9] He alerted three United employees, each of whom passed the buck, saying that they couldn't do anything about the situation. The next day, when Carroll discovered that the abuse had damaged his guitar, he began attempting to open a claim against United. After nine months of phone calls, emails, faxes, and frustration, United denied his claim. On his website DaveCarrollMusic.com, he wrote:

> At that moment it occurred to me that I had been fighting a losing battle all this time and that fighting over this at all was a waste of time. The system is designed to frustrate affected customers into giving up their claims and United is very good at it but I realized then that as a songwriter and traveling musician I wasn't without options. In my final reply to Ms. Irlweg [the representative who had issued the final denial of his claim] I told her that I would be writing three songs about United Airlines and my experience in the whole matter. I would then make videos for these songs and offer them for free download on YouTube and my own website, inviting viewers to vote on their favourite United song.

The first song, called "United Breaks Guitars," exploded onto the Internet, garnering over four million views by July 2009 (by December 2016, when I last viewed the video, it had over 16 million views). United finally offered to cover the repairs Carroll had undertaken on his guitar, along with $1,200 in flight vouchers, but Carroll declined, suggesting they donate the sum to charity instead. *The Guardian* later reported that other airlines had offered Carroll free trips so he could experience their customer service firsthand.[10] Meanwhile, United's share price took a 10 percent tumble as news of the debacle circled the globe.

Carroll hasn't let the matter drop. True to his word, he released two more videos, the last one in March 2010. He also released a book in 2012 called *United Breaks Guitars: The Power of One Voice in the Age of Social Media*. Its Amazon page describes it as "…a textbook example of the new relationship between companies and their customers [that] has demonstrated the power of one voice in the age of social media. It has become a benchmark in the customer-service and music industries, as well as [in] branding and social-media circles."

Visit DaveCarrollMusic.com/speaking, and you'll see that he still keynotes conferences and events around the world, spreading the story of how one person with a video camera and a cause shaved $180 million off the market valuation of one of the world's biggest companies.

Maybe nobody will create a YouTube sensation if your product or service isn't top notch; maybe someone will. Maybe nobody will blog about how your organization always goes the extra mile and how great you are to work with; then again, maybe someone will.

Everyone you encounter In the twenty-first century is a publisher and a marketer. "Just as Gutenberg's printing press did 600 years ago, blogs are democratizing the control of information and knowledge by diffusing it to a wider swath of people...If every blogger is a publisher, then every blog is also a platform—a stage in the middle of the virtual piazza. The challenge is to get the people to pay attention."[11] Getting everyone to pay attention is indeed a challenge. Everyone, including us, can produce something. But to get it in front of an audience, we must understand the changing dynamics of consumption and production. We must understand The Long Tail.

Long, Longer, Longest: Fragmentation at its Finest

> "The other thing that happens when consumers talk amongst themselves is that they discover that, collectively, their tastes are far more diverse than the marketing plans being fired at them suggest. Their interests splinter into ever narrower communities of affinity, going deeper and deeper into their chosen subject matter, as is always the case when like minds gather." Chris Anderson, *The Longer Long Tail* [12]

For those unfamiliar with the gist of The Long Tail, here's an explanation in Chris Anderson's own words:

Our culture and economy are increasingly shifting away from a focus on a relatively small number of hits (mainstream products and markets) at the head of the demand curve, and moving toward a huge number of niches in the tail.[13]

Such an idea is illustrated thus:

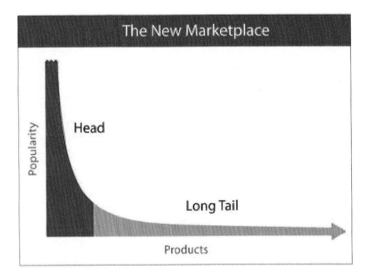

(image source: The LongTail.com)

The Long Tail is one of those ideas that, once you hear it, seems so obvious and intuitive that you wonder why you didn't think of it yourself. Well, don't worry; until Chris Anderson came along, no one else did, either. As editor of *Wired* magazine (and a wicked smart dude), Anderson was in the right intellectual place at the right cultural time to articulate the concept. Of course, it's not quite as simple as, "there are lots of people who like lots of different things." The reality of The Long Tail is more complex than that.

First of all, the potential of niches is meaningless until real people show up to populate them. So, even though "The Long Tail starts with a million niches," no one could effectively make use of those niches until warm human bodies could easily coalesce into them. We look to Anderson's six themes of The Long Tail for more explanation.

Theme #1: In virtually all markets, there are far more niche goods than hits. That ratio is growing exponentially larger as the tools of production become cheaper and more ubiquitous.

Anderson argues that the three forces of the long tail are "make it, get it out there, and help me find it." The only piece of that equation that differs from a pre-industrial community is the "help me find it;" putting a spotlight on your product, getting it to stand out in filtered social feeds or Google searches, now requires technical savvy. Stories abound of inventors whose brainchildren burst dramatically onto the scene with no help from search-engine optimization or social-media amplification. "Getting it out there" in your village and "getting it out there" on the Internet involve vastly different patterns of behavior, but the goals are similar.

As niche becomes norm, we need to remember what worked during similar historical moments. We can learn from the Industrial Revolution, TV's early days of lifestyle disruption, and the impact of cable. (Maybe we marched through marketing's roots for a reason! If you skipped the boring historical stuff, here's your cue to back up a few pages and review it.)

Theme #2: The costs of reaching those niches is now falling dramatically. Thanks to a combination of forces that include digital distribution, powerful search technologies, and broadband penetration, online markets are resetting the economics of retail. In many markets, it is now possible to offer a massively expanded variety of products.

Reaching a niche audience in the early days of radio and television would have been prohibitively expensive. The volume of people advertising could speak to was all that made it a viable system of distributing ideas. That dynamic contributed in turn to the creation of products designed to appeal to the largest possible percentage of people in that audience. As Seth Godin puts it, "Together these two principles—the idea that you can profitably interrupt consumers with ads and the idea that creating average stuff for average people at low prices is the way to defeat the competition—drove everything."[14]

In the era of The Long Tail, however, we can reach Shi Tzu owners and dachshund lovers with distinct campaigns designed to appeal to each of them. We must therefore create products and marketing messages that do the same.

Theme #3: Simply offering more variety, however, does not shift demand by itself. Consumers must be given ways to find niches that suit their particular needs and interests. Filters—a range of tools and techniques, from recommendations to rankings—do this well. They can drive demand down the Tail.

Bubbling to the top of searches and social-media feeds is a never-ending struggle for modern marketers, but these systems make it possible for us to do our jobs. When "customers have choices, they have to make decisions. And in order to make those decisions, they need information."[15] If we put ourselves and our brands in the position to provide that information freely and joyfully, we can funnel the demand down the Tail and toward our products.

Theme #4: Once there's massively expanded variety and the filters to sort through it, the demand curve flattens. There are still hits and niches. The hits are relatively less popular and the niches relatively more so.

This flattening effect translates to marketing campaigns too. Hit commercials that once made careers, like Apple's "1984" or Coke's "I'd Like to Teach the World to Sing," will become less impactful.

Instead, the niches—the YouTube channel and the printed publication—will draw in larger audiences. Throwing money at an enormous product launch will never again guarantee sales. A long-term plan of joining targeted niches as an interested member and contributing to communities before you want to sell them something will be the best (and possibly the only feasible) marketing strategy.

The prevalence and power of filters means that marketers must understand the technical components of our profession. Because algorithms govern our profession more than most, we'll be perpetually in crisis-management mode if we fail to anticipate filter changes.

Theme #5: All those niches add up. Although none sell in huge numbers, a collective of niche products can comprise a market rivaling that of the hits.

Communicating simultaneously with many communities is harder than shouting through a single commercial-shaped megaphone. But them's the breaks. Or, as my son's preschool teacher says, "You git what you git and you don't throw a fit." This is what we as marketers git, and there's no point in gitting ourselves bent out of shape over it. We can produce equivalent results for our organizations by going niche; and we may need to hire a few more people to do it effectively. More on this shortly.

Theme #6: Once all of this is in place, the natural shape of demand is revealed, undistorted by distribution bottlenecks, scarcity of information, and limited choice of shelf space. That shape, by the way, is far less hit driven than we have been led to believe: it's as diverse as the population itself.

Like our audiences, our marketing messages must become increasingly diverse. The answer to hyper-fragmentation is hyper-personalization, as evidenced by the current surge in popularity around account-based marketing (ABM). While more labor- and resource-intensive, these one-to-one, technology-centric approaches are now our way of life.

Of course, it all works because we can now fairly easily find these individuals and talk to them. Anderson believes that none of these themes will materialize "without one big economic trigger: reducing the costs of reaching niches."[16] Three forces combine to drive down the cost of communicating with conspiracy theorists and amateur DJs alike:

1. **Democratizing the tools of production.** Personal computers have put capabilities and tools from the printing press to the film studio in the hands of anyone passionate enough to learn to use them. In previous decades, a right of creative passage was to make your way to one of the centers of production—Los Angeles, New York, Paris. Now, the tools come to the talent. We, likewise, must go to our audiences. (They won't come looking for us.)[17]

2. **Cutting the costs of consumption by democratizing distribution.** The fact that anyone can make content has meaning only if others can enjoy the content. During the early days of radio, "anyone with a few dollars and some back issues of Popular Science could put a radio station on the air,".[18] However, the limited distribution range capped the demand a homegrown radio station could generate.

3. **Connecting supply and demand.** Introducing consumers to these new and newly available goods—driving demand down The Tail—is crucial. Early radio operators couldn't widely distribute their content, and they couldn't drum up demand for it.

The big takeaway from Anderson's groundbreaking work is not that we have countless audiences to mine; it's that our brands, and, by extension, their marketing, face a rapid decline in authority. We work in "an era of radical change...Faith in advertising and the institutions that pay for it is waning, while faith in individuals is on the rise. Peers trust peers. Top-down messaging is losing traction, while bottom-up buzz is gaining power...The same inversion of power is now changing the marketing game for everything from individual products to people. The collective now controls the message."[19]

Now that we have a more robust understanding of the historical roots of our profession, the similarities between the present and previous periods of prosperity become clear. Again, Theodore MacManus: "Eye fixed on the future, he scorned quick, spectacular campaigns aimed at fast sales. Instead, in the same unhurried way that two people became friends, he aimed to build a friendship based on a slow accumulation of favorable impressions."[20] One hundred years ago, it was clear to MacManus that he must woo his audience. The relationship, the atmosphere, the careful song and dance mattered to buyers who had the luxury of choice.

Thanks to The Long Tail's dynamics, marketers and advertisers will operate under similar conditions for the foreseeable future. For our own inspiration we must channel our inner MacManus (and his disciples such as David Ogilvy). The era of the hard sell, of the price-centric, undifferentiated products, has passed, possibly forever.

CHAPTER FOUR

Why Marketing Matters in a Hyper-Fragmented World

"If advertising persuades some men to live beyond their means, so does matrimony. If advertising speaks to a thousand in order to influence one, so does the church. If advertising is often garrulous and redundant and tiresome, so is the United States Senate. We are young, and law and medicine and theology are old." Bruce Barton

If you're the world's leading expert on grooming Shi Tzus, the advent of The Long Tail is great news for you. Now your blog, which you started as a passion project to share your knowledge with any audience other than your long-suffering spouse, has the potential to reach a like-minded peer group. You can even monetize your expertise by offering online courses, email newsletters, and virtual consulting; the possibilities are limitless.

To marketers, the advent of The Long Tail also presents opportunities, although it might not seem that way at first glance. If the digital revolution has turned everyone with a smartphone into a content producer, an influencer, and yes, a marketer, where does that leave professional marketers and advertisers? Why would a company hire an army of people to specialize in content creation, social-media amplification, lead nurturing, and all the other labels we assign to our daily tasks when the market is already running amok with the messaging? When the audiences can turn it into whatever they want?

For many reasons, a brand's success still relies on "real" marketers. The big reason is a many-headed monster: audience expectations.

Now that anybody with a laptop, tablet, or smartphone and an Internet connection can create a website, start a podcast, or record a video, these things have lost much of their luster and impact. As technology continues its march toward democratization, people increasingly have the means to contribute to conversations that were once rigidly controlled by gatekeepers. In order for their contributions to stand out, brands must do better. Much better.

Showing up is a given. Everybody has a ticket. Everybody knows the dress code. Everybody brought a gift for the host.

Brands and their marketing teams must arrive early, wear designer clothes, hand out an endless stream of top-shelf drinks, and seem to be selling nothing.

If the world's leading expert on Shi Tzus can run a blog, a podcast, and an email newsletter by putting in a few hours a week on the side, a pet-food label wanting to reach that niche audience must do something ten times as good. Marketers—good ones who understand the audience, its preferences, and creating what aligns with them—are the only ones who can do that.

Now that brands compete for audience attention against everybody who cares enough to share an opinion *as well as other brands*, it's harder than ever to reach people. Audience members passionate enough to be heard typically have no agenda. They don't push people to sign up for their newsletter the instant they land on a blog post; their social-media followers are at no risk of spam bombardment. To compete for minds and eyeballs, we'd better behave at least as well.

Do I need to point out that selling without seeming to do so is really difficult? My experience talking marketing with executives has taught me that it does. Let's make this perfectly clear: you want professionals managing this process.

With fragmentation happily splitting into hyper-fragmentation, you need forward-thinking teams of people who can and want to forge new paths to reach new niches in ways we can't imagine. Aside from remarkable dumb luck, understanding the audience and connecting to digital trends is the only way to make this work.

The rare marketer who foresees an emerging trend often gets treated like the kid who cried wolf. A percentage of the people reading this book no doubt tried to get their organization to jump on Instagram, Snapchat, or any of the shiny new communities that have emerged since I wrote this, only to be shot down.

Note to bosses everywhere: "New Media channels like blogs and social networks work in a completely different way. They don't succeed because a CEO embraces them. They succeed because individuals embrace them."[21]

If we succeed in getting permission to join an in-progress conversation, we're told to stay on message, maintain brand consistency, include the logo, and run it all by legal.

The problem is, this kind of behavior reeks of corporate self-promotion, and nobody in today's audiences abides that nonsense. When an audience can turn to any of the regular individuals who happily do cool stuff and ask for nothing in return, why would anybody care about our watered-down, legally-sanctioned, cookie-cutter messaging? As Chris Anderson reminds us, one of the most important consequences of The Long Tail is the shift from audiences "being passive consumers to active producers. And we're doing it for the love of it (the word "amateur" derives from the Latin amator, "lover," from, in turn, amare, "to love")."[22] When marketers aren't doing it for the love of a topic, when we're clearly in it for the conversion or the lead or the sale, it shows, and we fail.

Of course, this failure is not always (maybe even not often) marketing's fault.

The organizations where many of us work were established long before Snapchat, Pinterest, or even Facebook. They put down roots in traditional times and grew strong branches based on proven business models and tried-and-true marketing approaches. They produce what Seth Godin calls meatballs: "a commodity, a branded item of little differentiation and decent quality. We've always needed meatballs. Call them staples or commodities or the basic building blocks of civilized society, but we need them advertised, and we need them in quantity."[23]

Meatballs and Old Marketing, "the act of interrupting masses of people with ads about average products," go very well together. Founded on scarcity of choice and large reserves of cheap attention, Old Marketing is what advertisers employed throughout history. (Still haven't read Part One of this book?)

Now, thanks to the dynamics of The Long Tail and the fundamental disruptions of digital life, we find that audiences "need" products and services that are distinctly un-meatball-like. Marketing new products and services using old tactics simply can't work. Marketing meatballs using the old tactics doesn't work either.

In *Meatball Sundae*, Godin argues:

"At the same time that there are whole new ways to market, the tactics of building a business haven't caught up yet.

Marketers are trying to play a new game, but their co-workers are still busy playing the old one."[24]

Organizations that understand this new way of marketing rely on storytelling and remarkable products to differentiate ourselves in a noisy and crowded world. We market only to those who have given us permission to talk with them. In the first (2009) edition of *Meatball Sundae*, Godin identified fourteen trends of what he called "New Marketing." And—no surprise, if you've been following Seth Godin—they remain remarkably relevant and accurate eight years later. Here's his list:

1. Direct communication and commerce between producers and consumers
2. Amplification of the voice of the consumer and independent authorities
3. The need for an authentic story as the number of sources increases
4. Extremely short attention spans due to clutter
5. The Long Tail
6. Outsourcing
7. Google and the dicing of everything
8. Infinite channels of communication
9. Direct communication and commerce between consumers and consumers
10. Shifts in scarcity and abundance
11. The triumph of big ideas
12. The shift from "how many" to "who"
13. The wealthy are like us
14. New gatekeepers, no gatekeepers

Considering how utterly these circumstances differ from those we encountered historically, it's tempting to infer that people themselves have fundamentally changed. The needs and wants of a 2017 consumer who relies on online reviews to choose a restaurant seems to have little in common with the 1950s consumer whose dining choices were almost entirely determined by television commercials. But no; people remain the same. The environment has changed.

Paradoxically, this is what makes marketers so important. In a world where more and more people have enough disposable income to buy practically anything they can dream up, we can get what we've been after all along: "to be treated with respect and to be connected to other people."[25]

The simplicity of that want belies the complexity of executing marketing campaigns against it. Convincing someone to take a particular action while treating him or her respectfully and maintaining a meaningful connection is *hard*. Marketers who can do this are rare. If you are one, let me offer you a virtual fist bump. If you employ people with these skills, you may want to fly to Part Three right now so that you can start building an environment that keeps them around. Because they are the key—the only key—to building a successful organization in the twenty-first century.

"If marketing is at the core of every organization, and marketing is different," Godin reminds us, "then the organization that surrounds it must respond. Marketing doesn't support the organization. The organization supports marketing."[26]

It's easy to blame marketing failures on a poorly-adapted organization, but ultimately it doesn't matter whether that failure comes from an organization that hasn't evolved or from a marketer who just wasn't very good. It's still a failure that compounds marketing's persistent image problem. Because marketers and marketing still have a serious image problem. Despite our ever-growing power to influence the course of markets and brands, we're fighting the same battles for legitimacy that our predecessors fought a century ago (and we're not even selling Dr. William's Pink Pills for Pale People).

That Other Time Marketing Lost its Way: The Dot-Com Boom and Bust

Nowhere has marketing's image problem been more pronounced than during the dot-com boom and bust, when the industry abandoned its lessons and ideals to chase heaps of venture-capital cash. The industry still suffers from the fallout of this era, so we'll spend the last part of this chapter exploring the period.

Ushered in with the twenty-first century, the marketing excesses of the dot-com era reached absurd levels. In 1998, the top 50 Internet advertisers in the United States spent $420 million on offline advertising. In the *first two months* of 1999, dot-com companies poured $1.2 billion into that bucket.

Just as in Part One, when we explored the earliest challenges of marketing, our focus again falls not on internal brand-marketing teams but on advertising agencies, because most of the dot-coms clamoring for campaigns had no time to build their own teams. Given the breakneck pace at which the dot-coms ran in 1999, 2000, and into 2001, hiring marketing experts to build a brand from scratch wasn't an option. The agencies, "hypnotized by the venture capital cash being waved in their faces," lined up to sell their souls. They "agreed to shelve everything they'd learned about building brands in order to produce shallow, only occasionally witty advertising whose sole aim was to generate hyper-rapid awareness for their clients."[27]

Traditional advertising agencies were the primary beneficiaries of huge dot-com budgets for another reason: most of the dot-coms focused on print, television, and outdoor advertising, precisely where agencies already excelled.

Accustomed to dealing with executives from Fortune 100 companies like Procter & Gamble and Coca-Cola, "Bewildered middle-aged agency suits sat open-mouthed as teams of idiots in three-quarter length trousers and Japanese trainers hosed backers' money at them...They took their briefs from 26-year-old marketing directors whose sole previous experience had been the production of club fliers..."[28] To say that these inexperienced "marketers" made poor choices is a monumental understatement. According to an analysis conducted by the independent investment research firm Pegasus, sales and marketing expense rates in the dot-com sector ranged from 90 percent to 133 percent in 1999 and 62 percent to 95 percent in 2000. For example, in 1999, Stamps.com spent 98 cents on marketing per dollar of revenue. (In 2003, after the crash, that spend fell to 15 cents.)[29]

Examples abound.

Recall the E-trade Super Bowl ad from 2000; a dancing monkey and this voice-over: "Well, we just wasted 2 million bucks. What are you doing with your money?"

How about the Pets.com sock-puppet mascot, maybe the epitome of the dot-com disconnect between marketing dollars and business results? Created by San Francisco-based agency TBWA/Chiat/Day, the puppet was made of a white sports sock. Its felt eyes were mismatched, the ears were held on with safety pins, and a watch served as its collar. Like the puppet itself, Pets.com ads featuring their newly-minted mascot were "knowingly amateurish."[30] Each ad ended with the line, "Because pets can't drive." Like much dot-com advertising, the slogan was moderately clever, but did little to entice consumers into action. Of course pets can't drive. They couldn't drive yesterday before I saw this commercial, and they can't drive now. How is that information supposed to change the way I shop for pet supplies? It didn't.

Pet.com's sock puppet brought press coverage and no revenue. From an earned-media standpoint, the sock puppet was a huge success. It was covered extensively by the press and invited onto talk shows. It generated a line of merchandise. As Pets.com went under, the image of its mascot turned out to be the company's most valuable asset, and it was ultimately sold to a licensing company.

From a business perspective, the sock puppet was a huge failure. While consumers were happy to watch an entertaining sock puppet for 30-second spans during commercials, they continued to buy dog food at their neighborhood pet stores.

In 2000, Computer.com, a site designed to help novice computer users navigate their technology, blew 60 percent of its funding on 90 seconds of Super Bowl ad time. And it wasn't alone in its poor decision-making. *Salon*, in "Fumble.com," its post-mortem of the 2000 Super Bowl ad parade, didn't pull any punches:

> Having started with just $5.8 million in seed financing, you squandered more than half of your capital in less time than it takes to soft-boil an egg. Congratulations! That fancy caper puts your little start-up in the running for the hotly contested title of Fastest Dot-Com to Piss Away the Greatest Percentage of Its Funding. And now it's time to—what else?—dust off your pitch and raise more money! How excruciating it must be to meet

with potential investors, when the one thing your
company is known for—if it's known for anything
at all—is having the genius (or stupidity) to spend
money at the rate of just under $38,889 a second.[31]

More than a million bucks to air a 60-second ad, and that
doesn't include production costs. What did dot-com businesses get
for these exorbitant outlays? Perhaps a slight uptick in website traffic
and maybe some press coverage, but nothing as lasting as brand
awareness or as crucial as customers.

Seventeen dot-coms advertised during the 2000 Super Bowl.
How many do you remember?

- AutoTrader.com
- Britannica.com
- Computer.com
- Epidemic.com
- E-Trade.com
- Hotjobs.com
- Kforce.com
- LastMinuteTravel.com
- LifeMinders.com
- Monster.com
- Netpliance.com
- OnMoney.com
- Oxygen.com
- OurBeginning.com

- Pets.com

- Webex.com

- WebMD.com

In the days immediately following the Super Bowl, only 17 percent of people who watched at least three-quarters of the game could, with no prompting, name one dot-com company that had run an ad. For 11 of the 17 dot-coms that advertised during the broadcast, not even one viewer remembered seeing their ad.[32]

In yet another lesson about the need for long-term marketing commitment, the companies that released multiple commercials before the Super Bowl earned the highest brand recall. The big winner was E-Trade.com, with six percent of viewers remembering that they saw that ad.

Pets.com, our poster child for dot-com marketing idiocy, closed both its virtual and real-life doors in November 2000, not quite ten months after its multimillion-dollar one-day spend on the Super Bowl. Its investment capital of $300 million vanished as its stock price fell from the IPO high of $11 to 19 cents.

Images of the sock puppet were so widespread, and its inability to salvage the foundering company so well-known, that E-Trade referenced it during its 2001 Super Bowl ad. In the 30-second spot, a chimp rides a horse through a rundown dot-com town, passing an empty storefront for Pimentoloaf.com and an abandoned sports car with the license plate "DOT COMER" before stopping at a building with a sign for "Esocks.com." A wrecking ball crashes through the sign, throwing a sock puppet at the chimp's feet. The chimp picks it up, two tears silently rolling down its cheeks. "Invest wisely," the closing tag line implores.

Indeed.

A lot of people learned hard lessons from the dot-com boom and bust. For marketers, advertising agencies, and brands, the need to develop a real relationship with a targeted audience was painfully clear. Throwing money, even hundreds of millions of dollars, at marketing could not shore up a floundering business or build a brand overnight. Marketing had clearly become a long game that could not be won by a single big idea or one brilliant ad campaign. Many dot-com companies were founded on good ideas. Others were not. All failed when they neglected marketing (and management) fundamentals. Even in the unstable dot-com landscape and the early days of digital advertising, history could have shown them the way.

Had the dot-coms not committed the cardinal sin of ignoring the past, they might have profited from the straight-talking ideas of John E. Powers. As you may recall, he was one of the earliest advocates for clear language without hyperbole. His ad for the clothing company that was on the verge of closing its doors could have applied to many failing dot-coms in 2001:

> We are bankrupt. This announcement will bring our creditors down on our necks. But if you come and buy tomorrow we shall have the money to meet them. If not we will go to the wall.

Or they could have taken advice from the turn of the twentieth century, when Claude Hopkins pioneered the concept of a unique value proposition (although he called it a pre-emptive claim) saying, "You cannot go into a well-occupied field on the simple appeal, 'buy my brand.' That is repugnant to all. One must offer exceptional service to induce people to change from a favourite brand to yours."[33]

If Pets.com had told their audiences what was in it for them, if they had devoted time and energy into crafting a message that communicated the value of their service rather than going for the flashy mascot, they might have made it.

As our march through marketing history approaches the present, we'll look closely at how our image problem has played out in American marketing departments. We'll see how it has contributed to conflict between marketers and executives and led many marketers to check out of a game that seems unwinnable.

Before we embark on this slightly depressing chapter, I leave you with one last Seth Godin exhortation:

> It doesn't particularly matter whether or not you sell records or do recordkeeping, whether you surf the Web or sell surfboards. It's still the same math. Consumers are in charge. They're bored. They're narcissistic. And they certainly don't have the patience for your meetings or your strategy decks or your clueless CEO.
>
> First one in, doing it right, wins.[34]

CHAPTER FIVE

The Perils of Opinion-based Expertise

"You can't hire somebody because he says, 'Hey, I'm a consumer. I buy stuff. And I know a lot of people who buy stuff, so I know how to market.' People are not born marketers. They have to learn to be marketers, and they have to really want to be marketers."
Sergio Zyman, *The End of Marketing as We Know It*[35]

If the first one in, doing it right, wins, then doesn't it make sense to fill your marketing department with people who can do it right and see far enough into the future to get there first? Sadly, that does not reflect the prevailing wisdom. CEOs hear stories of twelve year-old YouTube sensations and overnight Pinterest phenoms and figure they'd rather be lucky than good. When marketing starts to sound like a roll of the dice, executives start to think that it must not matter who you've got rolling.

Even George Masters, the creator of the "Tiny Machine" video that we discussed earlier, had no formal training in marketing or advertising. As his video traversed the Internet on its unstoppable viral march, an analyst at Jupiter Research said of the piece, "You could take this thing and put it on MTV this afternoon. It's not only good, it's good advertising. People go to college to learn this. He just gets it."[36]

Maybe he did get it, or maybe he just happened to take a branded product as the subject for his video and that made him look like a natural advertising genius. If he had used an old Walkman or Discman for his video, would that analyst have assumed that he possessed some kind of innate marketing intuition? Probably not. Masters would still have great video production skills (which he acquired through extensive study and application), but he wouldn't be hailed as someone who "just gets" advertising.

If we're looking for a gambling metaphor, marketing is more like poker than craps. It matters who you've got holding your cards. The cards can turn bad for anybody, but knowledge of probability, the ability to read others, willingness to adapt, and a tolerance for risk distinguish both a good poker player and a good marketer.

If poker were only about the cards you're dealt, there wouldn't be professional players making millions of dollars every year; nobody's that lucky. Yet that seems to be the perception about marketers—we get lucky and our campaign goes viral, or Lady Luck turns against us and the latest experiment fails.

Instead, a campaign going viral is usually the result of careful planning, meticulous execution, and timing born of years of experience. Just as we don't see the thousands of hands professional poker players lose before they become the best in the world, we don't hear about the tests and trials that marketers embark on prior to any success.

When corporate profits skyrocket, executives don't presume that the CEO happened to be in the right place at the right time, but it's commonplace for a marketer's success to be ascribed to coincidence.

I used to think that my experience must be influencing my feelings about this topic. When I was outlining this book, I was on the fence about including this chapter. After all, I've never worked in a marketing department at a huge, multinational enterprise with thousands of employees. I imagined that in those types of organizations, marketing and marketers must get the respect (and the salaries) that they deserve. Surely, I said to myself, they hire qualified professionals and then allow them to do their jobs. How else could they have such effective marketing?

Then, while researching this section, I came across the *The End of Marketing as We Know It* (1999) by Sergio Zyman. Zyman ran marketing at Coca-Cola when they released New Coke in 1985 and then reintroduced Coke Classic 77 days later. He left the company shortly afterwards, ran a successful consulting business for several years, and then returned to Coke.

His book includes impassioned arguments for how to structure a marketing team, an account of his troubled relationship with advertising agencies, and more than one attempt to retell the story of New Coke. What struck me most was his insistence that marketing be treated as a legitimate profession:

> The future of marketing lies in establishing it as a professional discipline that is based on sound business principles and that produces sound business results...As long as marketing is viewed as a nonessential activity, and therefore an expense, executives will feel free to randomly cut marketing budget. This reduces its effectiveness and invites further cuts. It is a downward spiral to oblivion.[37]

The fact that Zyman felt compelled to make these arguments convinced me that this chapter belongs. If the guy who ran the marketing department for one of the world's most successful and admired brands had to fight to hire enough staff; if he struggled to position his craft as an actual profession; if he fought the tendency to throw onto the marketing team random employees who fit nowhere else; then clearly my career experience isn't an isolated incident.

As a group, marketers are suffering from the rise in opinion-based expertise, which is basically the perception that marketing ideas don't derive from education, experience, or data, but rather from someone's opinion. This phenomenon manifests itself in the belief that if you're a person who was ever influenced by marketing materials to make a purchase, then you're qualified to be a marketer. You may recognize this as "Let's get my nephew to build our new landing page" syndrome.

While annoying and unhelpful in marketing strategy sessions, the concept of opinion-based expertise has ramifications far beyond migraine-inducing meetings. For many executives, it has led to the loss of respect for marketing as a profession and marketers as professionals. The consequences of this point of view manifest in two problematic and incongruous ways:

1. **Unrealistic expectations.** Marketers are expected to be miracle workers who are capable of bringing in thousands of leads literally overnight because the CEO read something one time about how someone did that just by using this one pop-up form. The abundance of words like "tips," "tricks," "shortcuts," and "hacks" in articles about marketing work are all shorthand for "what we do isn't really that hard."

2. Willingness to slash budgets indiscriminately.
You'd think that if marketing could "increase web traffic by 2,000 percent by making one simple change," as dozens of online articles claim, our budgets would be huge and untouchable. Yet in many organizations marketing sits in the expense column. It's seen as a cost to be cut rather than a driver of growth and innovation. Again, if marketing expertise requires nothing more than an opinion, it can't be all that powerful.

This situation is just plain crappy. When done right, marketing is hard. Being good at marketing requires intelligence, creativity, and experience. But when our boss's bosses think our ideas are equivalent to those of their niece who posts pictures of her cat on Snapchat, or, even worse, that they can override our carefully considered tactics based on something they read somewhere last night, it is nothing short of maddening. At the end of the day, the "problem when relying on subjective criteria is that the marketer's opinion is at the mercy of the opinions of others. A more senior stakeholder's novice opinion can end up holding sway because marketers simply lack the firepower to extinguish such interference."[37]

Both of these manifestations contribute to marketers' current plight, leaving us to feel overworked and underappreciated despite the wins we rack up. But don't despair. In Part Three, we unravel this knot to reveal solutions.

World War C: Marketing vs. the C-Suite

One SaaS company had a particularly thorny relationship with marketing. At one point, they decided to eliminate onboarding sales. This seemed prudent, as inbound marketing had become so effective for them that they no longer needed those salespeople to sell anything. The company didn't want to fire employees who had done nothing wrong, but the fact remained that they had five employees who no longer had anything to do. Like many organizations, they decided to transplant them into the marketing department.

Congratulations! You're all marketers!

Thrown suddenly into a profession for which they had no training or experience, the former salespeople did their best, but they could not produce. As Sergio Zyman sees it, this kind of thing happens all the time in marketing:

> Because executives don't really understand marketing, they hire whatever bodies come along, or dump their brothers-in-law and the other people they don't know what to do with, into the marketing department. Fortunately some of them, especially the young kids who have the energy and the desire to learn, do a good job despite their initial lack of qualifications. But companies also end up with a lot of people in jobs for which they aren't qualified.[38]

Not too long ago, such behavior by the C-suite had little consequence. When most companies were shortchanging their marketing departments, "you could get by with just a few good marketers and a bunch of other people to answer the telephone and shepherd projects. But in the future, you aren't going to be able to get away with that. Every day, marketers have to do more and more and work harder and smarter."[39] That was written in 1999. Consider how much more complex and competitive your industry has grown since then, and you'll understand why throwing warm bodies at marketing requirements doesn't cut it.

Some see the technologization of marketing as a reason to hire people with software or product expertise and then teach them (or expect them to magically learn, perhaps by osmosis) the fundamentals of marketing. This poor excuse for thinking is epitomized by *The Accidental Marketer*, a 2014 book by Tom Spitale and Mary Abbazia. The promotional website for the book explains its purpose:

> You may be asking, just who is an Accidental Marketer? In today's technology-driven world, many businesses are hiring scientists, engineers, and designers to fulfill strategic-marketing and product-management roles. These are Accidental Marketers, untrained marketers now tasked with developing marketing strategies.
>
> The Accidental Marketer is a practical guide for these professionals. Through 10 marketing tools featured in the book, these Accidental Marketers will be given the immediate ability to create powerful strategies that increase sales and profits for any product in any industry.[40]

While this book takes a stab at demystifying the world of marketing for the uninitiated, its hyped-up promise does the marketing profession no favors. By telling potential readers that one book and ten tools can bestow upon them the "immediate ability to create powerful strategies that increase sales and profits for any product in any industry," Spitale and Abbazia are pouring fuel on the fire of opinion-based expertise. Who needs a decade of experience? Buy this book, read it real quick, and you're all set.

Of course, no competent manager would consider entrusting something as important as marketing to one of these shake-and-bake marketers. Right?

Wrong. Hiring managers, executives, and even marketing managers have hired "marketers" whose expertise extends no farther than consuming a few books like *The Accidental Marketer*. They grab employees who write clever emails, transfer them to marketing, and assume that it will all work out fine.

If a CPA left the company, can you imagine the company filling the vacant position with someone off the street, handing her a book called *The Accidental Accountant*, and expecting the company's financial health to remain stable?

How about a software developer? Would any company that builds apps or SaaS products or websites pull in someone from the mail room, put a few books on his desk, and expect him to deliver working code on Friday?

Of course not. These are professions that require training, experience, and no small amount of cleverness. Marketing is, too, yet a seemingly endless parade of articles and books like *The Accidental Marketer* purport to boil it down to its once-hidden essence. As they wind down their book, Spitale and Abbazia wax hopeful:

> We hope that as a result of reading this book, you are more empowered in creating your own strategy and marketing plan. Likely, *The Accidental Marketer* helped you realize that marketing strategy is more scientific and rational than you thought. That's what working with tools and frameworks can do: help you make sense out of brilliant strategies that previously seemed to be random acts of genius.[41]

Ten tools, a few case studies, a couple hundred pages, and poof! You, too, are a marketer.

Given this trend, it's not surprising that most C-suite executives report that they don't trust marketers any farther than they can throw them (and I hear of a growth hack that enables you to, with just one small adjustment, increase that distance by 50 percent).

In 2011 and 2012, The Fournaise Marketing Group interviewed hundreds of CEOs and decision-makers in North America, Europe, Asia, and Australia, asking about marketing's credibility and about executive trust in what marketing gets up to all day. The findings:

- 80 percent are "not very impressed" with the work that marketing produces.

- 73 percent think marketers lack business credibility and cannot demonstrate how their strategies and campaigns grow the business.

- 77 percent see a major disconnect between marketers' talk (brand values, brand equity, etc.) and the results that matter to CEOs, such as revenue, sales, EBIT, or market valuation.

- 74 percent believe marketers spend too much time focused on "the latest marketing trends such as social media but can rarely demonstrate how these trends will help them generate more business for the company."

- 73 percent find that marketers interpret calls for increased ROI as a demand to cut costs rather than generate more top-line growth in the form of sales, revenue, prospects, or buyers.

- 72 percent said marketing is always asking for more money without explaining how it will generate business.

- 70 percent feel bombarded by irrelevant marketing data that is unconnected to the company's profits and losses.

- 67 percent said their marketers don't think enough like business people, focusing too much on the "arty" and "fluffy" components of marketing and relying too heavily on agencies to generate their next big idea. [42][43]

On the other side, 69 percent of the marketers Fournaise spoke with believed that their strategies and campaigns made an impact on the company's bottom line, even though they weren't able to quantify that impact. "But," I'm sure many of you are thinking, "marketing is all about data now. Everybody is data-driven, and executives love data, so this problem will work itself out pretty soon."

Jerome Fontaine, CEO and Chief Tracker of Fournaise, agrees with you. In the press release that accompanied the 2012 study, he argued that, "People trust doctors, surgeons, lawyers, pilots or accountants: simply because they know these no-nonsense professionals are trained to focus on the right set of data to take the best decisions and achieve the best outcomes possible. CEOs trust CFOs and CIOs for the same reasons. It's not a game of data, but rather a game of the 'right and relevant' data for the right purpose and the right decision-making, with no fluff around."[44]

It would be easy and convenient to hail data as our savior, but recall Part One and the plain vanilla advertising that dominated the 1950s. One of the primary contributors to that bland and boring moment in marketing history was data. As agencies developed the ability to perform extensive market research, they focused on repeating what had once been successful rather than moving to new approaches that might perform even better.

Recall what Stephen Fox points out in *The Mirror Makers*. "Traditional advertising research, stressing quantified returns on old campaigns, had an implicitly conservative bias that typically urged a repeat of whatever had worked before." As a result, "most of 1950s advertising ... was safe and dull, without flair or distinction. The memorable ads seemed especially good because they had so little competition."[45]

There are many parallels between yawn-inducing ads of the 1950s and the endless sea of mediocre marketing in which consumers are currently adrift. DDB and the dozens of visionaries it launched broke through by breaking with convention, not by following The Ultimate Step-by-Step Guide to Marketing Cars. Like a great jazz ensemble, DDB's team riffed on convention, creating things that were conventional enough to be understood by their audience, but not so rote that they would fade into the background. DDB was the first, but by no means the only, "creative agency." It incubated enormous talents like Mary Wells and George Lois, both of whom eventually started their own agencies that contributed to the resurgence of a reliance on creative power to create impactful advertising.

Two decades later, in the 1970s, the cycle of marketing had turned once again. In both copy style and internal management, agencies in the 70s resembled their mid-century counterparts. A careful "student of advertising cycles might have predicted the trade's future...back to hard sell, science, and research...a shift from the creative departments to management, from little boutiques to bigness and mergers, from vivid personalities to corporate anonymity. In sum, a fast trip in a time machine back to the 1950s."[46] The results were uniformity and lackluster campaigns: "As in the 1950s, advertising lost creative verve when it regarded itself as a rational, quantifiable science."[47]

By understanding what's happened to our industry in the past, we're better equipped to deal with present challenges. History seems to tell us that while data can help bridge the legitimacy gap between marketing and the C-suite, it can't be the only thing that drives decision-making. While marketing prowess may not be derived from having an opinion, it *does* often come from being able to confidently follow an instinct into uncharted territory.

The reality of most of the "hacks" and "tricks" that fill our search results is that the people for whom they worked tried something new and unexpected that worked brilliantly for them. When they promote it in an article or podcast or online course, it seems like a simple trick because someone already did it and can show others how it works. But the first time somebody "hacks" something, there's no guarantee it's going to work. She followed her gut, took a chance, and it paid off.

The originator of this kind of hacking is arguably Mark Zuckerberg, whose S-1 registration statement for Facebook, filed with the Securities and Exchange Commission, included a section called "The Hacker Way." There Zuckerberg countered the common perception of what it means to hack something:

> Hacking just means building something quickly or testing the boundaries of what can be done...The Hacker Way is an approach to building that involves continuous improvement and iteration. Hackers believe that something can always be better, and that nothing is ever complete. They just have to go fix it -- often in the face of people who say it's impossible or are content with the status quo... Instead of debating for days whether a new idea is possible or what the best way to build something is, hackers would rather just prototype something and see what works.[48]

Without this reliance on intuition born of experience, marketing risks once more slipping into repetitive stagnation. But this time, we're marketing to people who have hundreds of ways to spend their time. This isn't the 1950s audience who could count their entertainment options without using their toes. If we start leaning too heavily on data and get boring, or even slightly less entertaining than the video of a baby goat their friend just sent them, our audience goes somewhere else.

That's why the "tools and frameworks" promised by books and articles like *The Accidental Marketer* make me grind my teeth: following the same steps that everyone else is following is going to take you to exactly the same place—a boring place where nobody wants to buy what you're selling. If you want to get somewhere new, you've got to find your own path. Data might help show you the way, but relying on it exclusively isn't going to help you walk it.

Jay Acunzo, host of the podcast "Unthinkable," explores the paradoxical relationship between data and creativity on his show and in his writing. In one post titled "Confessions of a Content Creator: I Don't Care About Data," he writes:

> What's the ROI of my work? I proudly can't tell you. I can tell you that everyone in the market we're trying to reach can't get enough of our stuff. I can tell you that human beings like good things that make them feel good. But can I say, "42?" No. And I don't care.

The short-term thinking. The tips and tricks and secrets. Our obsession with this stuff — because we have to measure it and get results right now— prevents us from admitting what we all should have admitted when the phrase "content marketing" first emerged:

This is about making great art.[49]

Mending the rift in marketing's relationship with CEOs and VPs is important. Marketing has never been better positioned to make overtures in that direction. But if we sell out our creativity for a handful of magic data, we'll be mindlessly churning out copycat work that destroys our souls, alienates our audiences, and turns us into the marketing undead. Time is running out to make this change; this tragic fate has already befallen many marketers.

Saving Yourself From the Zombie Marketer Apocalypse

You've no doubt encountered them at some point during your professional life. Despite existing in a seemingly constant state of panic and disarray, they never seem to really see what's going on around them. Then, in complete contrast to their frenetic scurrying, they stare, dead-eyed and unmoving, for hours at the blinking cursor on their computer monitor.

Many marketers have succumbed to the stresses outlined in this chapter. They go through their days like zombies, doing rote, repetitive work without creativity or enthusiasm. They are the marketing undead.

They're not simply an urban legend or a story that marketers tell new hires to keep them in line. Whether it's the never-ending battles with executives for legitimacy, the 24/7 schedule required by social media, or the publish-or-perish demands of content marketing, causes for zombification abound. In this final section we take a hard look at marketers: what we report about our own working lives and what others say about us. We need to fix this situation firmly in our minds, because it's what we'll counteract with an influx of Agility in Part Three.

Our first stop is the *European Journal of Marketing*, where a report titled "The Depiction of Marketing and Marketers in the News Media" gives us insight into how marketers appear in newspapers. Author Robert Cluley reviewed 6,877 documents drawn from three national newspapers in the United Kingdom over two one-year periods. As he suspected when he began the study, marketers' portrayal in the news media does little to change our reputation as manipulative snake-oil salespeople. In summarizing his findings, Cluley writes that "marketing is rarely discussed in accordance with the definitions of marketing set out by industry bodies" such as the Chartered Institute of Marketers or the American Marketing Association. "Instead, marketing is most regularly used to refer to sales and advertising practices and with little recognition that marketers take account of consumer needs."[50]

One of the most intriguing observations in this paper comes in the conclusion, where Cluley posits that "the marketing profession may suffer as individual marketers successfully achieve their objectives."[51] This paradox makes sense if you consider other writing about marketing that emphasizes marketers' tendency to use psychology and emotional triggers to "make" people buy things. As an example, check out this excerpt from a 2013 article for *Psychology Today*, "How Marketers Manipulate You Without You Knowing" by Douglas Van Praet:

Consumers can be both negatively and positively predisposed to a brand based on their unconscious associations with its ads, slogans, logos, mascots, design elements, and brand properties. People may not really know why they love one brand and not another, because conscious thought may have had little to do with the emotional tags that were formed when their preferences were learned. For example, a leading beverage company created a sound when opening the can that was subtly different from other cans to trigger a unique craving for their brand's drink. The manufacturer redesigned the can to create a differentiating snapping sound, a branded cue of delicious anticipation. They then recorded the sound in a studio and incorporated it into advertising. The manufacturer would play the sound at major concerts and sporting events, seeing an instant uptick in sales for their brand when they did so. Yet when consumers were asked why they suddenly choose that particular beverage over another they would say things like "I haven't the faintest idea, I just fell for it." [52]

The marketers who came up with the idea to change the sound a can makes when it's opened are pretty clever. They're delivering results for the business and doing their jobs well. On the other hand, they didn't do anything to make the product better. They simply made a small adjustment to its container that would drive more people to buy it. Although these individual marketers were successful in their efforts to move more beverages, marketing takes a hit. Based on this type of coverage, you might conclude marketing hasn't changed too much since the days of mixing turpentine, alcohol, and red pepper and selling it as a miracle cure.

Despite the majority of news reports covering the success of individual marketing practitioners, those practitioners are typically portrayed as sources of authority only during times of turmoil for their organization. Cluley found that "marketers were positioned as a source of authority in 47.5 per cent of the reports,"[53] providing details about the companies they work for, the products they sell, and the markets they target. Some stories even included general advice from marketers based on their expertise, such as advice suggesting that job seekers market their personal brands to land a better position. Far less common were instances of marketers listening to their audiences, with only 7.3 percent of stories including a mention of marketers receiving information.[54]

What I find interesting in these results is that when things go well—when we succeed in convincing people to buy a product or be loyal to a brand—marketers are labeled as manipulative. Simultaneously, if there's a mishap on Twitter or a public-relations fiasco, we're always first in line when it comes time to receive blame.

Consider the marketing minds behind a blog post, created by The Humane Society of Silicon Valley, about a Chihuahua named Eddie the Terrible. The post, which includes illustrations that insert Eddie into ads for *The Walking Dead*, *American Horror Story*, and *Breaking Bad*, is brilliantly written:

> While Eddie The Terrible has never actually attacked another dog, he's made it abundantly clear that he hasn't ruled out the possibility. He goes from zero to Cujo in .05 seconds when he sees another dog on leash.

Want your kids to grow up with a full complement
of fingers and toes? Not the dog for you.

While Eddie is crate trained, he has a weird thing
about sleeping in the crate. And by weird thing we
mean 'nope, not happening'. A bed in your room?
Awesome. In the bed with you? Better. In a crate?
Let him sing you the song of his people…[56]

The post got 143 comments and coverage on *The Huffington Post*
and delivered on the Humane Society equivalent of a conversion,
enticing a nice couple to take Eddie home. The adoption brought in
additional coverage from *Good Morning America* and *Inside Edition*, as
well as an uptick in donations for the shelter.

But here's the kicker: the Humane Society had been creating
similar posts long before this one by Finnegan Dowling went viral.
They were devoted marketers doing exemplary work, fighting the
good fight, never becoming the marketing undead, and it eventually
paid off. And yet when quoted by the *Huffington Post*, Dowling is called
a spokesperson for the HSSV, while Ann Handley (a fellow marketer)
cites Dowling's job as social-media manager for the shelter.[57]

Marketers, it seems, get no respect even when they manage
to get a demonic Chihuahua adopted. Surely, there's no way a
profession that relies on psychological manipulation to get me to buy
a particular beverage could simultaneously manage to do something
so heroic!

The Humane Society is heralded as the clever originator of
the campaign; the writer of the blog post is a spokesperson, not
a social-media manager. Marketers share stories like this amongst
themselves—I heard Eddie's story at a marketing conference—but

the general public tends to overlook the fact that marketers save puppies and kittens every single day. We *are* superheroes.

This lack of credit and surfeit of blame could certainly be enough to turn a wide-eyed young marketer into a disillusioned zombie. But wait, there's more.

It's not just the general public that makes marketing a challenging field to work in. Our colleagues and workloads do their part to up the difficulty level of our days. The most recent U.S. State of Marketing Work Report, released by Workfront in late 2016, paints a bleak picture of marketers' days.[57]

Forty-hour workweeks appear to be a thing of the past, with marketers reporting they work 45.9 hours per week on average (the average for non-marketers was 45.1). During those hours, a meager 27 percent take a full hour for lunch; 54 percent take 30 minutes or less, with 16 percent saying they don't take a lunch break at all. Most people (46 percent) are too busy to take their allotted lunch break, while others say they prefer to work through lunch.

You might think that if we're spending so much time with our noses to the marketing grindstone we'd be cranking out campaigns constantly, but it turns out that we spend just over a third of our day—38 percent—performing our actual job duties. We lose 17 percent of the day to email, nine percent to wasteful meetings, and eight percent to interruptions for nonessential tasks.

If you were working 45 hours a week but still couldn't keep up with your workload or hit your targets, wouldn't you employ every single tool at your disposal to get things done? Marketers are simply people who, like everybody else, want to keep their jobs. When we're stretched too thin, we sometimes resort to desperate measures. In reality, all professionals and knowledge workers do this. On Friday at 5:30 p.m., everybody wants to get out the door; many of us are willing to turn in sub-standard work to make that happen. The difference is that when marketers do it, hundreds, thousands, or even millions of people see our work. When we succumb to internal conflicts, unreasonable deadlines, or outdated expectations from our bosses and become the marketing undead, it affects everyone who encounters the marketing messages we produce.

I think we can do better than that.

I propose that, by making individual marketers less stressed and more efficient at their jobs, we can raise the caliber of the marketing they produce. This may help us change the conversation around marketing as a profession. If we can spend the majority of our professional lives listening to and engaging with our audiences and creating marketing materials they'll enjoy, consumers will encounter less irrelevant, low-quality, interrupt-driven messaging.

Marketers' workdays will be more fulfilling and less frantic. Organizations will reap the benefits that come with more effective marketing, including increased revenue, reduced costs, and more brand loyalty.

Everybody wins.

PART THREE

Agile to the Rescue

"Previously, [marketing] was a relatively narrowly defined function, was often well integrated with the rest of the firm, was at arm's length from real customers, was run with a yearly or quarterly rhythm, that relied on a standard set of tactics, and was generally resistant to change. Today, it is a faster-moving, more innovative engine of growth that thrives on direct customer engagement, adapts to disruption, and is strategically entwined with the entirety of the business."
Scott Brinker, *Hacking Marketing*

Having traveled through nearly 150 years of marketing history, our current situation should feel fairly familiar. In the 1920s, marketing and distribution replaced production as the natural limit on industrial activity. Now, as the digital age makes distribution less cumbersome, marketing gains even more influence in deciding which products, brands, and ideas succeed. During the 1950s and 70s, data displaced creativity, resulting in advertising campaigns that were lackluster in both their creativity and business outcomes. With marketing automation, analytics on everything, and increasing demands for demonstrable marketing ROI, the danger of forfeiting the artistic side of marketing for a few more sales again looms.

Brands looking for overnight marketing magic still risk going the way of the dot-com boom.

Marketing remains a long game best played by professionals.

It should be clear by now that even though modern marketers have our own unique challenges, adopting a deliberately historical perspective reveals ongoing themes. These similarities show us that the primary principles of effective marketing have changed very little, meaning that we have an even larger pool of case studies and role models to draw from.

There are, of course, significant differences between how modern marketing functions and the way it did for our predecessors. Channels have multiplied. Audiences have fragmented. Technology makes everyone a marketer. Cycles of innovation and irrelevancy last weeks instead of years.

What does this new reality mean? The fundamentals don't change much, but the way we construct and execute our marketing campaigns must change completely. The "what" of marketing is the same; we have to overhaul the "how."

If we don't make ground-up changes to how we manage marketing, how can we hope to keep pace with an ever-fragmenting audience who no longer relies on advertisers, marketers, or brands? If your marketing team doesn't get it right, someone else—a competitor or even an amateur—will. When I, fixated on pushing my product, lumber into a conversation among enthusiasts, I don't merely fail to generate results for my client. I erode the already-frayed relationships between my peers and all of their audiences.

For over a century, irrelevant, meaningless, ineffective marketing campaigns have damaged cultural perceptions of our industry. Our stature within our organizations steadily diminishes. Heads roll, leaving those who keep their jobs with longer workweeks, but less time to do good work.

You lose. I lose. We continue to look like the bad guys. The cycle continues.

How do we change the narrative? How do we take back our work? By radically changing the way we play the game. But what does that look like? Again, we look to history—recent history. At the turn of the millennium, software developers found themselves in a downward spiral that looked a lot like ours. A handful of thought leaders, unwilling to watch their profession crash and burn, gathered on the literal mountaintop to find a way out of the tailspin. In 2001, they *creat*ed their salvation and gave it a simple and wonderfully descriptive name: Agile. Their solution can also works for us.

We can save ourselves, but the transformation from the historical marketing industry to an Agile one requires commitment and no small amount of courage. And instead of leaving the hard work to the top one percent of marketing teams—Google and GE and Proctor & Gamble—we all have to walk the walk. Marketing departments, agencies, and individuals have to blaze our own unique trails to Agility.

And we need to get started right away. The handful of marketing teams that have figured this out are producing highly relevant, real-time marketing messages. They're wowing their audiences. They're impressing their bosses and their clients. They're getting results. As long as we rely on our old-school, predictive playbook, we'll continue to look bad. Really, really bad.

You know the predictive approach I'm talking about: you figure out exactly what you need to do to achieve a goal, estimate how long it will take you to do all of it, and start working. This approach worked when we fully understood the requirements and scope of a project and when the nothing changed once the work had begun. But even in the old days, how often did that happen? Pretty close to never.

Projects went over budget, expanded far beyond their original scope, and crushed team members beneath their weight even without trying to target a hyper-fragmented audience scurrying across a complex digital landscape. And now, our markets and today's audiences are in constant flux. Even if our initial planning could be completely accurate—and it can't—by the time we execute that perfect plan, our campaign could be obsolete and irrelevant.

Agile marketing is built on the assumption that we can't know everything upfront, so we must be flexible while executing our plan. It's known as an adaptive approach, and it's ideal in an environment of uncertainty.

There isn't a clear demarcation between predictive and adaptive approaches to marketing. Both approaches fall at points on a continuum, and you're likely to find yourself using parts of each as you execute marketing plans in our complex reality. Black-and-white choices may be simpler, but just as early copywriters took their inspiration from both Hopkins' common-sense, reason-why approach and MacManus' friendly, low-pressure suggestion style, modern marketers must create their own Agile formulas.

What I present here is not a template for an Agile quarterly plan or a step-by-step guide to running an Agile marketing team. In this final section, my goal is to give you all the information you need to start making a change for the better.

The hardest part of most journeys is the first step. I hope that, when you finish this book, you're inspired to take a first, confident step towards Agility.

CHAPTER SIX

Agile Methodologies for Marketing

"The terms 'Agile' dates back to a 2001 conclave where I and sixteen other leaders in software development wrote up what has become known as the 'Agile Manifesto.' It declared the following values: people over processes; products that actually work over documenting what the product is supposed to do; collaborating with customers over negotiating with them; and responding to change over following a plan. Scrum is the framework I built to put those values into practice. There is no methodology." Jeff Sutherland, Scrum

I have a secret to share: I kind of hate the word "methodology." There's nothing wrong with it from an etymological or phonetic perspective, but when I talk to people about which Agile methodology they should choose, their eyes instantly glaze over. A methodology somehow sounds simultaneously boring and complex.

Agile marketing methodologies don't have to be either.

A methodology is simply the system we choose to help us manage the day-to-day logistics of marketing. It is what we *do* to support our larger goal of being Agile.

Each major Agile methodology—Scrum, Kanban, Scrumban, and Lean—has its own best practices. We'll get into those soon. For now, you want to identify the methodology, tool, or system that constantly improves your team's Agility. In other words, the point of adopting Agile marketing is not to get better at Scrum or to become a more expert Lean practitioner. It's to increase our alignment with the values and principles outlined in the Agile Marketing Manifesto so that we become better, more Agile marketers.

Written in 2011 and based on the original 2001 Agile Manifesto for software development, our manifesto includes seven values and twelve principles that should form the foundation of any and all implementations of Agile marketing.

Agile Marketing Values:

1. Validated learning over opinions and conventions
2. Customer-focused collaboration over silos and hierarchy
3. Adaptive and iterative campaigns over Big-Bang campaigns
4. The process of customer discovery over static prediction
5. Flexible vs. rigid planning
6. Responding to change over following a plan
7. Many small experiments over a few large bets

Agile Marketing Principles:

1. Our highest priority is to satisfy the customer through early and continuous delivery of marketing that solves problems.
2. We welcome and plan for change. Our ability to quickly respond to change is a source of competitive advantage.
3. Deliver marketing programs frequently, from two a month to six a year; two per month is better.
4. Great marketing requires close alignment with the business, sales, and development people.
5. Build marketing programs around motivated individuals.

Give these individuals the environment and support they need, and trust them to get the job done.

6. Learning, through the build-measure-learn feedback loop, is the primary measure of progress.

7. Sustainable marketing requires you to keep a constant pace and pipeline.

8. Don't be afraid to fail; just don't fail the same way twice.

9. Continuous attention to marketing fundamentals and good design enhances agility.

10. Simplicity is essential.[1]

Most of these concepts are not revolutionary on their own. But taken together and combined with a system that allows you to put them into practice as you design and execute marketing plans, they are immensely powerful. That's where methodologies come into play; they guide us in turning words into daily practices. "Because," as Scott Brinker puts it, "although it's nice to aspire to be agile—as a generic synonym of *nimble*—to actually achieve that agility requires concrete changes to the way we operate."[2]

Scrum for Marketing

"Whenever people are involved in a complex, creative effort, whether they're trying to send a rocket to space, build a better light switch, or capture a criminal, traditional management methods simply break apart." Jeff Sutherland, *Scrum*[3]

When they hear the phrase "agile marketing," most people think of Scrum. It was the original Agile methodology for software, and it still gets the most press. It was developed in the late 90s by Ken Schwaber and Jeff Sutherland, who pioneered the system to address huge problems in the world of software development. Featuring timeboxed sprints, clearly defined roles, and multiple required ceremonies, Scrum is one of the most popular—and most prescriptive—frameworks for transitioning a team to Agile.

Before Agile software development and Scrum came along, development teams tried to produce functional, useful software based solely on massive requirements documents. These tomes were supposed to contain all of the requirements for the software or feature, but they never did. New things always came up during the development process that increased the size of the project; you know this phenomenon as scope creep. Developers themselves often underestimated the complexity and difficulty of their work; they had become all too familiar with the whooshing sound of another deadline flying by.

Incomplete requirements, scope creep, and overlooked complexity all rained down on development teams, creating projects that were over budget, late, and barely functional. It's not hard to see why they were desperate for a new mode of operating.

The original goal of Scrum was to embrace the uncertainty and creativity that already governed software development. "At its root," Jeff Sutherland believes, "Scrum is based on a simple idea: whenever you start a project, why not regularly check in, see if what you're doing is heading in the right direction, and if it's actually what people want?"[4] (See what I mean by Agility being based in common sense?) To make those simple goals possible, Scrum provides a framework that creates a culture of transparency, inspection, and adaptation while making it easier for team members to produce consistently great products.

That framework has two basic parts: events and roles. The events, also referred to as ceremonies, create a regular, predictable cadence for Scrum teams. They include:

1. Sprint Planning
2. Daily Scrum (also known as Daily Standup)
3. Sprint Review
4. Sprint Retrospective

Scrum events translate fairly easily from a software team to a marketing department. The second half of Scrum—the roles of the people who occupy the framework—doesn't adapt nearly as well. Typical software Scrum roles are:

1. Product Owner
2. Scrum Master
3. Developers

Most marketing teams who adopt Scrum as their methodology of choice adjust the roles; we'll get to that soon. By keeping the components of Scrum that work well (events) and adjusting those that don't apply (roles), we can arrive at a framework for marketers that enables us to creatively and effectively use Scrum. Let's start with the events.

The Scrum framework consists of four formal events: Sprint Planning, Daily Scrum, Sprint Review, and Sprint Retrospective. Here's an overview, drawn from my experience, the Scrum Guide, and Jeff Sutherland's *Scrum*, of how to structure these ceremonies.

Note that each event has a purpose within the Scrum methodology. In the early days of adoption, it can seem like you spend all your time managing the process. You may be tempted to ax one or more of these meetings, but give them a chance before you cut them out. "Each event presents a formal opportunity to inspect and adapt," the Scrum Guide reminds us. "Not including an event will risk losing transparency and missing opportunities to improve the Scrum process."[5] I'm not the Scrum police, so I won't come haul you off to Scrum jail if you eliminate your Sprint Reviews. Chop components if you must, but only to improve your process and performance.

Sprint Planning

Sprint Planning is just what it sounds like. You get the team together to make a plan for what you can get done during your next Sprint. To keep things manageable and releases rapid, Sprints always last less than four weeks. Experiment to see what Sprint duration makes sense for your team and then stick to that; it doesn't work to set a one-week Sprint and then a three-week Sprint.

During the meeting, the entire marketing team creates the Sprint Plan based on what's at the top of the Backlog, the prioritized to-do list that governs the work of all Agile marketing teams. The creation of the Backlog can be a group effort or the responsibility of a single person, but it typically happens through collaboration between a marketing manager, marketing VP, or other leader, and a representative of the marketing team, most likely a Product Owner (or equivalent).

While stakeholders create the contents of the Backlog based on business goals and departmental priorities, the Agile team chooses when and how to accomplish that work.

A key outcome of the Sprint Planning meeting is the Sprint Goal, the primary objective of the coming Sprint. For marketing teams, the Sprint Goal can focus the Sprint on completing a project or a shippable piece of a long-term initiative. Without the Sprint Goal, it's easy to fixate on completing one-off tasks that don't help achieve larger marketing goals. Keep in mind that a Sprint Goal "can be any other coherence that causes the [Marketing] Team to work together rather than on separate initiatives."[6] Remember that! Team members often work simultaneously on disparate tasks and projects. Sprint Goals can remind us that we're all driving together to one finish line.

At the end of the Sprint Planning meeting, the team commits to completing their chosen amount of work within the coming Sprint. This should be a formal process of agreement, because it's now the team's responsibility as a group to get all that work done. No one should be able to change or add to their workload once the Sprint has begun. This team sanctity is one of the most important pillars of Scrum, particularly in the interrupt-driven world of marketing, so make sure executives and other departments are clear about your team's Sprint Goals and what work they've committed to completing.

How to Know How Much You Can Do:
The Estimation Enigma

An obvious question comes up at this point: how does a team know how much work they can do in one Sprint? To figure this out, you need to estimate the size of the work in the Backlog to know how much your team can realistically handle during the next few weeks. Jeff Sutherland recommends never trying to estimate in hours, "because people are absolutely terrible at that."[7] Instead, he suggests estimating by relative size, such as t-shirt sizes: x-small, small, medium, and large, or with the Fibonacci sequence: 1, 2, 3, 5, 8, 13, 21.

The Fibonacci sequence is often more helpful than t-shirt sizes because there is more distinction between the estimated sizes. A size-two project or task is exactly one-quarter of a size eight; the difference between a small project and large project is entirely arbitrary and subjective. (You can mitigate this lack of precision by assigning numerical values to the t-shirt sizes: x-small is a one, large is an eight, and so on; but then you might as well use Fibonacci.) I should say, however, that many Agile marketing teams ultimately settle on using hours to estimate the items in the Backlog. The practice may not be completely in line with Scrum's principles, but hours often turn out to be the most intuitive way for marketers to size their tasks. Experiment with work-estimation methods to see what works best for your team and its typical projects.

After a few Sprints, data tells you how much work you've done. You want this value, known as the team's Velocity, to increase consistently, which is why you spend time on task estimation. If your Velocity starts to dip, it's time to take a look at process and team performance to see what's changed or needs to change. If your team experiences external interruptions that impact Velocity, objective data shows you the real-world consequence of outside forces on your Sprint.

Finally, estimating your marketing work enables you to track the team's ongoing output with a Burndown Chart, which displays the number of points needed to complete the Sprint vs. the number of days left in the Sprint. Ideally, you plot a steep downward slope that simultaneously crosses zero on each axis.

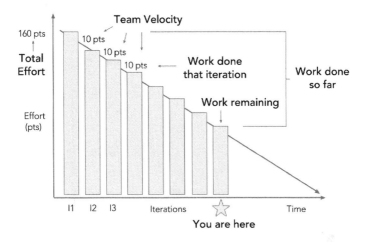

Getting the Most Out of Standup Meetings

The second Scrum event, and one of the most powerful in the whole methodology, is known as the Daily Standup or Daily Scrum. It takes place every day during a Sprint, is attended only by those who contribute directly to reaching the Sprint Goal, and features each team member discussing his or her progress and impediments. It's strictly timeboxed to 15 minutes, a limit to be enforced by the Scrum Master. During this Daily Scrum, each team member outlines:

- What they did yesterday to contribute to achieving the Sprint Goal
- What they plan to do today to contribute to achieving the Goal
- Barriers—individual or team—that threaten the Goal

Strictly speaking, no one who is not on the marketing team or directly contributing to the Sprint Goal(s) should attend the Daily Scrum.

Because team members rarely work on just one thing, it can be a challenge for each one to stay engaged while others share their updates. To counteract this common problem, follow Jeff Sutherland's suggestion to approach Daily Standups more like a football huddle than ticking boxes on a checklist:

> A wide receiver might say, "I'm having a problem with that defensive lineman," to which an offensive blocker might respond, "I'll take care of that. I'll open that line." Or the quarterback might say, "Our running game is hitting a wall; let's surprise them with a pass to the left." the idea is for the team to quickly confer on how to move toward victory -- i.e., complete the Sprint. Passivity is not only lazy, it actively hurts the rest of the team's performance. Once spotted, it needs to be eliminated immediately. I want aggressive teams -- ones that come out of the daily meeting knowing the most important thing they need to accomplish that day. One person will hear another say that a task will take a day, but another team member might know how to do it in an hour if they work together. I want teams emerging from that meeting saying things like, "Let's nail this. Let's do this." The team needs to *want* to be great.[8]

Sanctioned Showing Off in the Sprint Review

Sometimes called a Sprint Demo, this meeting happens at the end of a Sprint once the work has been completed. Unlike Sprint Planning and Daily Scrum meetings, Sprint Reviews are open to anyone who wishes to attend. The team shows off what they achieved during the Sprint, including content, social-media posts, email campaigns, and new ads. This is not the time for quality assurance or edits; instead, it's a moment to review work that's completed and approved. You can share any preliminary performance data that you've collected on work that was released earlier in the Sprint.

Sprint Reviews often result in changes to the Backlog as stakeholders in attendance make adjustments based on what they see. They might want to adjust priorities to further iterate on an unexpected success, or they might choose to pull the plug on a dud in the backlog.

Finally, conduct your Sprint Review with an eye to your upcoming iteration. Spend time considering next steps for any projects to be included in future Sprints. For example, if you create one branch of an email nurture campaign and plan to add another during an upcoming Sprint, discuss and document any lessons from this iteration that might improve execution of the next. During the Sprint Review, look at changes in the marketplace, departmental priorities, budgets, or timelines so that they can be incorporated into future Sprint Planning.

Focus on the Team with the Sprint Retrospective

The final piece of Scrum is the Sprint Retrospective, a vital meeting in which the Scrum team inspects itself and its processes for opportunities to improve. Hold this meeting after the Sprint Review and before the next round of Sprint Planning, because outcomes from the Retrospective (sometimes abbreviated as Retro) almost certainly impact the next planning meeting. Again, the Retro isn't just about preparing to plan; it's about creating and using a safe environment in which the team does the hard work of identifying ways they can improve and where they can grow as a unit. Post the Retrospective Prime Directive somewhere in the Retro meeting room:

> Regardless of what we discover, we understand and truly believe that everyone did the best job they could, given what they knew at the time, their skills and abilities, the resources available, and the situation at hand.[9]

Traditionally, the Sprint Retrospective is structured around three questions: What should we stop doing in the next Sprint? What should we start doing? What should we continue doing? However, while these questions are helpful in launching an initial discussion about how the team can continuously improve its process, asking them during every single Sprint Retro can quickly lead to stagnation. Here are a few alternative ideas to help you mix things up. Simply shifting the questions around can generate new insights:

1. Ask, "What went well? What went poorly? What should we change?"
2. Have everyone describe the past sprint in one word by writing it on a sticky note. Then go around and ask each team member to explain why he or she chose that word.
3. What's something that caused problems last Sprint? If you could change one thing, what would it be? What don't we know yet?
4. What did you Like, Lack, Learn, and Long For during the past iteration?
5. Break down topics of discussion into what made the team Mad, Sad, and Glad.

Regardless of the structure you use, make sure that every member of the team has plenty of room to contribute. People who are uncomfortable speaking up may not work to make their voices heard, so the Scrum Master (or whoever is facilitating the meeting) needs to help them. Asking everyone to write their thoughts down on sticky notes first and having them share in turn can prevent dominant personalities from taking over the meeting.

Make sure that your intense discussion culminates in some action that can be incorporated into the next Sprint. To be effective, the concept of process improvement, also known as the *kaizen*, requires concrete, measurable changes. It frustrates a team to spend hours coming up with ways to function more effectively if, Sprint after Sprint, nothing changes.

A Word About Sprints Themselves

They sound like something fancy, but for marketers Sprints are simply discrete periods of work done to achieve an objective. Some teams structure their Sprints around completing a campaign or finishing a piece of a larger, ongoing project, but you need only ensure that the team is working on the most important set of tasks.

In the software world, each iteration exists to produce a *potentially* shippable piece of code, one that functions well enough to be released. There's no requirement to ship, or even release, at the end of each Sprint.

For marketers, each Sprint is an opportunity to rebalance priorities and adjust the plan based on new information. Since we work in a fast-paced digital world, systematizing this practice is enormously powerful:

Overall, the management metabolism of short sprints isn't about working harder or faster. It's about dynamically reallocating our efforts more frequently, to take advantage of new information and innovations more quickly than quarterly or yearly plans permit. Yet it lets us do this in a considered and balanced manner, avoiding a chaotic, interrupt-driven frenzy. That's agility.[10]

Adapting Scrum Teams for Marketing

So far we've stayed pretty true to the Scrum practices created for software development teams. Sprint Planning, Daily Standup, Sprint Reviews, and Retros all work much the same for both. But when it comes to team members, we need to make more significant adjustments to make Scrum work for marketing.

Software Scrum teams consist of a Product Owner, the Development Team, and a Scrum Master. The Scrum Guide states how these teams function:

- Self-organizing teams choose how best to accomplish their work rather than being directed by others outside the team.

- Cross-functional teams have all competencies needed to accomplish the work without depending on others not part of the team.

- The team model in Scrum is designed to optimize flexibility, creativity, and productivity.

The functional ideals of self-organization and cross-functionality apply, and we optimize our Agile marketing teams for flexibility, creativity, and productivity. However, our team structure often differs. Consider this diagram from Scott Brinker's *Hacking Marketing*:

11

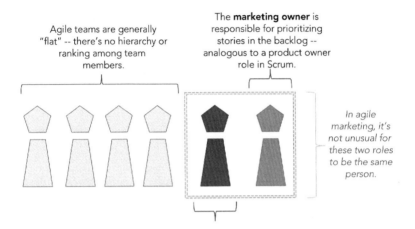

Agile teams are generally "flat" -- there's no hierarchy or ranking among team members.

The **marketing owner** is responsible for prioritizing stories in the backlog -- analogous to a product owner role in Scrum.

In agile marketing, it's not unusual for these two roles to be the same person.

Agile teams work best without hierarchy among the team members. But someone, traditionally the Scrum Master, needs to manage the process of continuous improvement. We also need a liaison with stakeholders outside the team who manages the contents of the Backlog, a function usually filled by the Product Owner.

Scott suggests changing the Product Owner to a Marketing Owner, a title that makes more sense on marketing teams that aren't actually producing a product. In the case of the Scrum Master, most marketing organizations lack the resources, if not the will, to dedicate someone's entire day to managing the Scrum process. The Marketing Owner may do double duty, serving as both the protector of the Backlog and the process facilitator as illustrated above. Alternatively, the responsibility may shift, monthly or quarterly, from one team member to another. Moving Scrum Master responsibilities around like this can help team members who are new to the Agile experience more fully understand how the process works and why it runs as it does. It's also an opportunity to get a new perspective on the process and how it could work better for the team.

Don't worry about getting each and every team certified as a Scrum Master if you plan to migrate the role; a basic understanding of Scrum principles is all you need to get started.

Choosing Your Scrum Team Size

The traditional formulation for Scrum team sizing is seven, plus or minus two. Anything larger and coordination becomes too difficult. The team—especially a distributed team whose members aren't all in the same office—falls out of sync and camaraderie and shared ownership fade. Departments too big to fit into a single team can form multiple Scrum teams based on project types (website, content, social media) audience segments, products, stages of the buyer's journey, or whatever cross-functional groups help you achieve the greatest velocity.

Smaller teams can also work—Jeff Sutherland says he's seen Scrum work teams as small as three—but lighter-weight methodologies like Kanban work better for teams of that size.

Kanban for Marketing

At the core of Kanban lies a paradox: by limiting the amount of work we do, we become more productive. When you consider how much time we lose to multitasking (or more accurately, task switching, since no one can truly multitask), you can see why this seemingly paradoxical methodology is so useful.

Compared to Scrum, Kanban is a young work-management method. In 2013, David J. Anderson best articulated its application to software development in his foundational book *Kanban: Successful Evolutionary Change for Your Technology Business*. Its adoption hasn't been as universal as Scrum's during the early days of Agile software development, but for teams that chafe under the strictures of the Scrum process, Kanban can serve as a freeing alternative.

Although it was adapted to knowledge work only a few years ago, the concept of kanban (lower case k) has been around for decades. The Japanese term "kanban" translates to "signal card" and was originally developed by Toyota in the 1940s. Inspired by grocery stores, which stock only as much product as people need, Toyota's manufacturing teams began using cards, or kanbans, to signal to other parts of the production line that they needed more parts. The use of kanban was part of a JIT (Just in Time) approach that enabled plants to create only as many parts as were needed at the time, and to conserve resources by not making extra.

Let's say my job is to put tires on a car. It's wasteful for me to have hundreds of tires that I don't yet need piled up behind me. It's efficient for the team that makes tires to produce them just in time for me to install them on a car. So once my stock reaches an agreed-upon point, say a dozen tires on hand, I put out a kanban card to spur the tire-making team to action. Throughout the assembly line, "workers at each step in the process are not allowed to do work unless they are signaled with a kanban from a downstream step."[12]

When applied to software development and marketing, a Kanban implementation doesn't typically include physical signal cards that cause another worker to begin work. Instead, the signal to pull new work is inferred from the visual quantity of work-in-progress in any given state. For example, if I'm responsible for editing content on my marketing team, I infer from the amount of work in the "waiting to be edited" column that it is or isn't time to pull a new project into my own workload. (This assumes that the number of items in progress in the "editing" column falls below the set WIP limit, enabling me to pull in additional work; more on that shortly.)

Ready (8)	Research/ Prep (2)	Create Ready	Creating (4)	Edit Ready	Editing (2)	Review Ready	Review (2)	Pub Ready

Like Scrum, a Kanban implementation requires a prioritized Backlog or to-do list from which the team pull their work. Business owners and stakeholders are responsible for religiously maintaining and prioritizing that list, because it is the sole source of work for the marketing team. You've probably seen kanban tracking boards used on all kinds of teams, but simply having a Backlog and moving work from one side of a whiteboard to another doesn't mean you're using Kanban. Anderson reminds us that "card walls are not inherently kanban systems. They are merely visual control systems. They allow teams to visually observe work-in-progress and self-organize, assign their own tasks, and move work from a backlog to complete without direction from a project or line manager. However, if there is no explicit limit to work-in-progress and no signaling to pull new work through the system, it is not a kanban system."[13]

Putting a bunch of cards on a wall doesn't mean you're using Kanban. In fact, many Scrum teams use this type of visualization to manage their work. The primary piece that sets Kanban apart is the commitment to limiting work-in-progress (WIP). Instead of using timeboxes to govern their work, as a Scrum team does, a

Kanban team uses WIP limits. Each state of work has an upper limit of productive work that it can contain. After the team exceeds that limit, waste enters the system. That upper limit then becomes a formalized piece of the Kanban process.

WIP limits vary from team to team and from one state of work to another. For example, your team of five might have a WIP limit of 10 on their "Doing" column, enabling each person to work on two things at once. The limit on work being reviewed, however, might be different, depending on how long this piece of the workflow takes, how many people are assigned to review work, and other factors. To ensure that your Kanban system functions at its highest possible level, routinely experiment with your WIP limits and document the outcomes.

Five Core Properties of Kanban

WIP limits may be Kanban's core defining feature, but they're not all you need. Anderson defines five core properties that make for a successful implementation:

1. Visualize Workflow
2. Limit Work-in-Progress
3. Measure and Manage Flow
4. Make Process Policies Explicit
5. Use Models to Recognize Improvement Opportunities

Unlike Scrum, Kanban doesn't prescribe a way of managing work; it doesn't dictate regular meetings or create unique roles within the team. Kanban assumes that you already have some form of work-management process in place, and that you want to continuously improve it. This makes Kanban easier than Scrum for marketing teams to implement, because you can start Kanban with little educational overhead.

Kanban also adapts readily to changing contexts. No two teams, even within the same department, implement it in exactly the same way. This makes sense: the bottlenecks in each team's workflow are distinct, so each team's improvement strategy is distinct. For Anderson, this approach is freeing:

> Kanban is giving permission in the market to create a tailored process optimized to a specific context. Kanban is giving people permission to think for themselves...You have permission to try Kanban. You have permission to modify your process. You have permission to be different. Your situation is unique and you deserve to develop a unique process definition tailored and optimized to your domain, your value stream, the risks that you manage, the skills of your team, and the demands of your customers.[14]

If you're new to Agility and aren't yet ready to think for yourself, this may sound terrifying rather than freeing; you might start with a Scrum implementation before moving toward Kanban.

Visualizing Flow with Your Kanban Board

The first rule of creating a Kanban board is that it must reflect reality rather than the official or ideal process for completing work on your marketing team. Your first task is to identify the start and end points for your team. Where do you take over complete control of work, and where do you hand it off to another team or department? These mark the beginning and end of your workflow visualization.

Next, fill in what happens on the team between those two points. One way to visualize how work makes its way through the team "is to think of any significant gates or gatekeepers in your workflow—such as approvals, reviews, handoffs from one person to another, or releases out into the world—and use those to define the columns of your board. Another approach is to think of parts of your workflow that have limits as to how many tasks can be in the same stage at the same time before your effectiveness in getting them all done begins to degrade."[15]

At its simplest, a marketing Kanban board can start with five columns: To Do, Create, Review, Test, and Done.

To Do	Create	Review	Test	Done

You may find it useful to sketch the flow organically, without trying to fit it into the vertical column view, before translating it into this format. The first few weeks are likely to see lots of changes to your board layout, so don't stress about getting it perfect the first time. Use a format that can easily be changed, such as dry-erase markers and sticky notes on a whiteboard. Once you're confident that the illustrated flow reflects your team's flow, you can create a more permanent version with tape or software.

Depending on the type of work your team typically does, columns for work that has left one state and is waiting to be pulled into the next may be useful. Known as buffers, these columns can help some teams visualize bottlenecks.

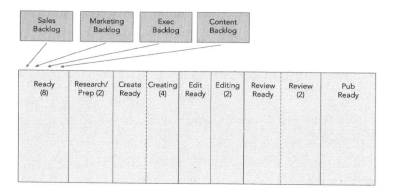

This sample content marketing board, for example, includes columns for content that is ready to be created, ready to be edited, ready to be published, and ready to publish.

When setting up your Kanban board, don't be too restrictive with the WIP limits you place on each column; make them a little higher than you need. Your workflow will be plagued by variability, waste, and bottlenecks early on, and you don't want those problems to interfere with the introduction of a pull-based mentality. As opportunities for improvement become clear, you can reduce WIP limits and add buffers accordingly.

Meetings and the Kanban Cadence

The daily standup meeting is an integral part of Kanban just as it is in Scrum, but the format deviates slightly. The Kanban board's accurate representation of all work in progress eliminates the need for team members to give daily status updates. Instead, the meeting centers on how work is (or isn't) flowing through the system. A facilitator of some kind walks the board, usually from right to left, reviewing the cards and, when need arises, querying team members for a status update or information that the team does not already have. A Kanban standup focuses on blocked items (a status that indicated on the card with a flag) or on cards that haven't changed status in several days.

This condensed style of standup is one reason that Kanban teams can be considerably larger than Scrum teams. Teams as large as 50 can complete these kinds of standups in under 15 minutes, a rate not feasible using the Scrum standup format.

Many Kanban teams also engage in what's known as an After Meeting, an informal gathering of team members who are collaborating on their own projects. Anderson reports that this ceremony "emerged as spontaneous behavior because team members wanted to discuss something on their minds: perhaps a blocking issue, perhaps a technical design or architecture issue, but more often, a process-related issue."[16] As a result, After Meetings tend to be fertile ground for ideas to improve process and generate innovations.

In place of Review and Retrospectives, Kanban teams use queue-replenishment meetings to keep their backlog prioritized and refined. They must happen at regular intervals, but their cadence doesn't need to be tied to any other cycle of Kanban. Even if you release new content every week, your queue replenishment might need to occur only once a month. Whatever timing you choose, make sure that it's consistent, because "a steady cadence for queue replenishment reduces the coordination cost of holding the meeting and provides certainty and reliability over the relationship between the business" and the marketing team.[17]

Whenever possible, include a variety of decision-makers from the most senior management position available in queue replenishment. These attendees can often provide more contextual detail and make decisions where lower-level attendees would have to defer. The goal is to produce a Backlog from which the marketing team can work with the utmost confidence, so you need attendees that can make that happen during the meeting.

Six Steps for Succeeding With Kanban

If you choose Kanban as your first Agile marketing methodology, keep in mind that the "essence of starting with Kanban is to change as little as possible," and that you want to map your existing workflow and processes before you begin the ongoing improvement efforts.

This recipe for success comes from David Anderson, who crafted it based on his experience as a new manager adopting an existing team. For marketing teams looking to adopt this methodology, these steps serve you equally well:

1. **Focus on Quality:** Anderson focused on this step first to cut down on the amount of time a development team spends dealing with software defects; marketers would do well to start here too. Without a commitment to producing the highest possible quality of marketing work, it doesn't really matter if you can enhance your productivity.

2. **Reduce Work-in-Progress:** There is a direct correlation between a lower WIP limit and an increase in quality, so this second step must be implemented along with, or immediately after, Step One. Reducing the amount of work that the team and its members do at any given time lowers

the time it takes to complete work *and* improves its quality. Keep your WIP as low as possible. Period.

3. **Deliver Often:** Frequent releases of content, email, social-media posts, and pretty much any other marketing collateral you can think of builds trust with audiences and stakeholders. They also increase the number of learning opportunities for your Agile team.

4. **Balance Demand Against Throughput:** In this step you're focused on finding a rate for accepting new work into the marketing Backlog that corresponds with the rate you can deliver high-quality marketing work. This is effectively limiting the WIP for your Backlog, and it means that discussions about priorities and commitments to completing new work can happen only after some work has been released. This balance produces some slack in the team's capacity. Only those working in the bottleneck areas are constantly busy, and even they mustn't feel overwhelmed. Slack is powerful because it enables team members to focus on doing their jobs with precision and quality and gives them time to apply themselves to improving the team and its workflow. This step can be difficult because we tend to want to optimize our workflow to use up everyone's available time. However, Kanban's continuous improvement demands a system with some slack, which can only be achieved by balancing demand against throughput.

5. **Prioritize:** When you have no predictability in your team, prioritization doesn't much matter, which is why it's down here at Step Five. But when high-quality work is going out steadily and the team has some slack in their days, management can begin to ensure that the most valuable

work is being done. Additionally, for marketing teams that lack political capital in an organization, building up confidence by showing an improved workflow may need to precede any attempt to change strategy or priorities.

6. **Attack Sources of Variability to Improve Predictability:** Variability is undesirable because it results in more WIP and longer release cycles. But understanding its effects and how to reduce it are advanced and difficult topics. When you've reached a high level of Agile maturity, you can tackle this final step by experimenting with your existing process policies.

Scrumban for Marketing

If Kanban is the adolescent member of the Agile work management family, Scrumban is the wee toddler. Although the foundational work on the methodology, Corey Ladas' *Scrumban: Essays on Kanban Systems for Lean Software Development*, was published in 2008, it hasn't yet caught on in the software world. Don't let this scare you away from giving Scrumban a try! Because it's still emerging, we have a chance to make our voices heard before its practices become as solidified (some might say fossilized) as those of Scrum.

While Ladas wrote the original book on Scrumban, a more helpful guide to its actual implementation was recently released in the form of Ajay Reddy's 2016 publication *The Scrumban [R]Evolution: Getting the Most Out of Agile, Scrum, and Lean Kanban*. This should be the foundational document for any marketing team looking to roll out this method because it's far more practical than Ladas' work, and includes case studies and examples. (Software case studies, yes. We can still learn from them.)

Although its name is obviously a combination of Scrum and Kanban, Scrumban isn't just about mashing together a few pieces of each methodology and calling it something new. Reddy defines it as "applying kanban systems within a Scrum context, and layering the Kanban Method alongside Scrum as a vehicle for evolutionary change. Ultimately, it's about aiding and amplifying the capabilities already inherent in Scrum, as well as providing new perspectives and capabilities."[18]

Scrumban emerged to fill gaps in both the Scrum and Kanban methodologies, which seem obvious in retrospect. Scrum covers meetings and roles in detail, but it does little to provide guidance on *how* teams should go about completing the work they commit to in each Sprint. It focuses on managing the project and the team, but not tasks themselves.

Kanban concentrates on the completion of individual work items. It assumes that some form of project-management system is in place on a team, and promises only to improve existing systems, not to create them.

For thinkers like Ladas and Reddy, putting the two pieces together just made sense.

Five Steps to a Scrumban Adoption

Because we've already covered all the foundational pieces of Scrumban, we can jump to steps for adoption. Remember, we're applying the Scrum structure to our team, and we're using Kanban to manage the flow of work.

Step One: Visualize Your Current System

Once again, remember that you're creating a visual representation of your current system, not the one you wish you had. It won't be perfect, and it might not be pretty, but this is a crucial step in rolling out Scrumban to your marketing team. The whole team participates in this step; no fair having a manager or director lay out the way they think things work. The goal is to identify these four key elements:

1. **Inputs:** The kind of work coming in to the team, including where it comes from. Input sources include other departments, executives, and customers.

2. **Process steps:** The stages of discovery or refinement through which work passes from the time the team accepts it to when it's considered complete. "Complete" might mean published, submitted for review, or something else for your team, and it might vary based on the type of work being done.

3. **Work performed outside the immediate team:** If you share resources with other teams, require approval from other departments, or rely on outsourced work, be sure to document that in your initial visualization.

4. **Outputs:** The team's completed work, including where and to whom it goes. Maybe this is a live website, or maybe you hand it off to development for publication. Capture the final phase of your work's lifecycle here.

If you're struggling to get a handle on a generalized workflow, it can be helpful to have each team member go through the exercise for two or three items he or she currently has in progress. Discuss how the work came into the team, what the team member is expected to do, and what's likely to happen once his or her work is done. After you do this a few times, you should start to see patterns that you can translate into a visual diagram something like this:

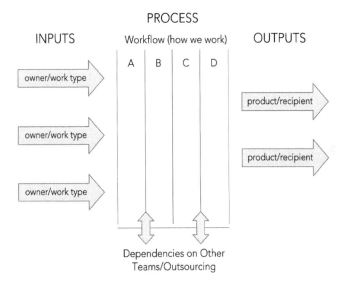

Step 1.5: Workflow into Kanban Board

Time to create your first working Kanban board. You can start with a physical or a virtual board, whichever works best for your team configuration. (Co-located teams more readily maintain a physical board than do dispersed teams.)

When designing your first Kanban board, make simplicity your guiding principle—simple, not vague. You get better results if you push for more something more specific than three columns labeled "To Do," "Doing," and "Done." If you need a jump start, refer to the five-column Kanban board illustrated in the previous section.

Fill your board with your current workload, and you're all set.

Step Two: Measure Your Performance

These four steps take place in the context of real work, so move items across your board, from left to right, as their status changes. The board belongs to the team, not to the manager or Scrum Master (if you have one), so each person is responsible for keeping his or her tasks current.

After a day or two of warm-up, start capturing and understanding these basic, important Scrumban metrics:

Amount of work in progress (WIP): Work that's been started but isn't finished yet. To arrive at a good starting point, divide the number of items the team is working on by the number of members on your team to get an average amount of WIP per person. So if you've got 42 items being worked on and seven people on your team, you've got an average WIP of six per person. Talk with your team: how does this number seem to them? Too much? Too little? Just right?

Blockers: Things that keep an item from moving to the next stage on the kanban board. Look at the work that's currently blocked and discuss how it got there. Are blockers more common in some parts of the process than in others? How long do items stay blocked? After only a few days you may not yet have much data so revisit it as issues arise.

Lead time: How long it takes an item to travel across the board. The team can break this down by item type (blog posts vs. social-media campaigns, for example) or plot the times on a histogram to see what's going on. Tracking lead time shows you how long it takes your team to complete each type of work, and it shows where to adjust if the lead time increases. Don't neglect this metric! The ability to accurately measure lead time for your system builds trust with stakeholders.

Throughput: Items completed in a given period. Marginally helpful at first, this metric becomes valuable when you need to determine whether changes you make to the system are having the desired impact.

Step Three:
Introduce WIP Limits for Focus and Stability

Scrumban principles state that we have to stabilize a system before we can improve it. Again, look to WIP limits to do this easily.

We can eventually apply WIP limits based on the system's actual capacity. Until then, applying random limits can be very revealing. Recall that WIP limits restrict the number of items in each column of your Kanban board; if you hit the WIP limit for work that's "In Progress," you can't start another project until you complete one.

Here, three states have limits; Done and Accepted don't need them:

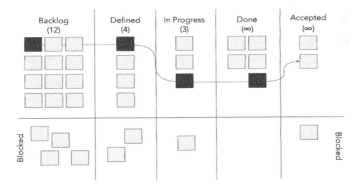

Step Four: Improve Your Understanding
and Management of Risk

While this is a very powerful component of Scrumban, understanding and managing risk can complicate early adoption efforts unnecessarily. To keep things simple at first, consider quantifying only the cost of delay.

When unplanned work is introduced onto the team, track its impact on work in progress. Did throughput drop? Were more items blocked until the fire drill was completed? Were marketing opportunities missed due to delayed releases?

Delay costs are real and significant, especially for marketers in competitive industries. Taking time to monitor the costs can arm you with a data-driven foundation for pushback against "emergency" work that isn't.

Step Five: Continuously Improve

We're talking only about the initial adoption phase, but your long-term goal is to continuously improve your process through regular experimentation and iteration. As Reddy puts it, "Teams should continuously seek process improvements, and continuously improve their ability to identify and prioritize the efforts most relevant to the capabilities they want to improve."[19] Part of the process is to help team members adopt habits and thought processes that enable them to embrace this mindset.

Coaches and Scrum masters can help by guiding teams to conduct basic experiments, such as attacking average lead time, by adopting a new team policy on blocked work items. They can also help to identify and avoid patterns of unsafe change.

You'll notice that there's no mention of Sprint Planning, Reviews, or Retrospectives in this five-step list. A Scrumban team may incorporate the purpose and function of those meetings into other components of their systems, or they may choose to modify them or omit them. While Scrum requires the inclusion of each ceremony for the methodology to function as intended, Scrumban encourages teams to break things when doing so helps them work more effectively.

Marketers always break things when they implement Scrum, a methodology designed for software teams. It's never going to work perfectly for us, so using a methodology designed to accommodate adjustments seems prudent.

A Note About Lean Marketing

The "Lean" philosophy is about identifying and eliminating sources of waste. Less waste leads to higher quality and lower costs, resulting in better business results. Derived from the Japanese manufacturing industry in general and Toyota's approaches in particular, Lean principles center on systematically removing three types of waste: non-value-adding work (*muda*), overburden (*muri*), and unevenness (*mura*). These support a focus on keeping work easy to understand, simple to do, and simple to manage, and a focus on workers embracing waste-reduction tools and appreciating the value of being Lean.

In its ultimate form, a Lean organization gets the right things to the right place at the right time and in the right quality to achieve perfect workflow, while minimizing waste and being flexible and able to change. Easy, right?

Leading theorists and practitioners of Scrum, Kanban, and Scrumban acknowledge the impact of Lean thinking on their methodologies, so we look briefly at that here. Lean principles underpin much of Agile thinking. Agile marketers find them a helpful supplement to any work-management methodology we choose, but Lean alone doesn't typically provide enough structure to transform a marketing department.

Although most marketing references to the Lean approach are based on Eric Ries' 2011 bestseller, *The Lean Startup* (which since its publication has inspired many startups and launched an entire business-management movement), the roots of reducing waste and staying lean go back further. Some believe that the term first appeared in the 1988 article "Triumph of the Lean Production System" by MIT student John Krafcik. Other sources cite Dr. Jim Womack, who has since authored the book, *Lean Thinking*, as the originator of Lean principles during his time in MIT's International Motor Vehicle Program.

But most famously, in 2011 Ries identified an intersection between Lean ideals and launching a new business. He offers five principles of the "Lean Startup:"

1. **Entrepreneurs are everywhere.** Startups are really just "a human institution designed to create new products and services under conditions of extreme uncertainty."
2. **Entrepreneurship is management.** "A startup is an institution, not just a product, and so it requires a new kind of management specifically geared to its context of extreme uncertainty."
3. **Validated learning.** Startups exist "to learn how to build a sustainable business." They do this best by running continuous experiments.

4. **Build-Measure-Learn.** There are three fundamental activities in which startups should be engaged: build products, see how customers respond to them, and learn whether to persevere with those products or pivot to something else.

5. **Innovation accounting.** The "boring stuff," like measuring progress, establishing milestones, and prioritizing work, is crucial for startups.[20]

The ideals of Lean operation and an Agile mindset are often conflated. Consider the five Principles of Lean articulated by the Lean Enterprise Institute:

1. Specify value from the standpoint of the end customer by product family.

2. Identify all the steps in the value stream for each product family, eliminating whenever possible those steps that do not create value.

3. Make the value-creating steps occur in tight sequence so the product will flow smoothly toward the customer.

4. As flow is introduced, let customers pull value from the next upstream activity.

5. As value is specified, value streams are identified, wasted steps are removed, and flow and pull are introduced, begin the process again and continue it until a state of perfection is reached in which perfect value is created with no waste.[21]

We saw a lot of that during our look at Agile methodologies; the two schools of thought are closely aligned.

I see no value in debating what to call the systems that can most effectively guide marketing teams into a digital, audience-driven future. Agile marketing and Lean startups are grandchildren of manufacturing ideas that originated in 1940s Japan. They share ancestry, aims, and many other elements. There's no need for us to bicker over language.

For example, a 2012 Hubspot article titled "Lean Marketing: How to Run Your Marketing Team Like a Startup" provides advice for how to run your marketing team like a Lean startup. Its suggestions include Agile methodologies:

- Organize Around the Sprint
- Structure Your Scrum Teams
- Create User Stories
- Commit to a Daily Standup[22]

When it comes to how we implement Agile marketing, naming conventions are irrelevant What matters is that we get ourselves out of old mindsets that do not serve us, our teams, or our audiences, adapt in real time, meet audience expectations without working all the time, and continuously realign with ever-changing business goals.

Choosing the Right Methodology for Your Team

We've barely touched on how these four methodologies—Scrum, Kanban, Scrumban, and Lean—function on a real team, but you now know enough to make an informed choice and get started. As you improve your Agility and engage in the all-important practice of kaizen, or continuous improvement, you'll want to expand on the basics. The citations at the end of the book tell you where all my information came from. You can attend in-person trainings and workshops (mine are outlined at the end of this book), and you can find marketing associations and conferences with Agile education on their agendas. Continuous improvement requires continuous education, so no resting on your Agile laurels once you've completed an initial adoption.

If you're curious about what others are doing, it's a mixed bag. VersionOne has, for years, been conducting a survey of Agile software developers; their latest results show that Scrum is by far the most common in this group:

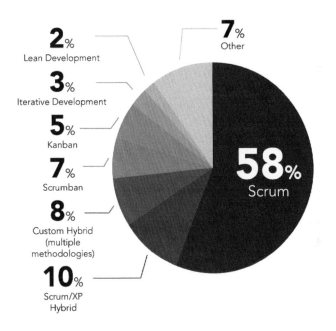

It's worth noting, however, that 39 percent of the respondents reported using Kanban within their organization as an Agile *technique* rather than a *methodology*. In their commentary on the results, VersionOne hypothesizes that this may indicate a future transition to "more flow-based methods such as Lean and Kanban" rather than the iteration-centered Scrum methodology.[23]

When it comes to marketing, the data is less clear and based on a much shorter historical period. A 2016 report from Workfront asked marketers, "What kind of work-management process does your marketing department use to manage work?" It received the following responses:

- I don't know: Two percent
- None: Five percent
- Take them as they come: 14 percent
- A combination of multiple methodologies: 40 percent
- We plan all the needed steps in a campaign at once, then execute the plan: 26 percent
- We deliberately re-organize our upcoming work based on feedback: 14 percent

The commentary on the report noted, "From question to question, the numbers of marketers who identified with Agile principles shifted significantly. The same was true of those who identified with more traditional work management principles. This points to the strong possibility that marketers are assembling their own piecemeal work methodologies."[24]

Another 2016 survey, this one from Wrike, asked marketers point-blank about their methodological leanings:

Which of the Agile methodologies best describes what your team uses?

- Lean. Eliminate non value-added work or steps; optimize the "system" for work; deliver as fast as possible: 29.7 percent

- Kanban. Team members pull work from a backlog; limit Work-in-Progress (WIP); continuous releases; visualize the workflow: 24.5 percent

- Scrumban. Team members pull work from a backlog; daily Scrum meetings if needed; visualize the workflow; limits on WIP; less emphasis on defined sprints (can include continuous releases); 14.5 percent

- Scrum. Regular, defined sprints; work is planned in advance; Daily Scrum meetings (or standups); retrospectives for improvement; no new work added during sprints: 13.8 percent

- A mix: Some or all of the above: 17.3 percent

- Other: .1 percent

While Lean and Kanban are the clear leaders and Scrum comes in last of the named methodologies, there seems to be little consensus from marketers about which work-management system they prefer.[25]

This is challenging for those of us hoping to help shepherd in a more Agile future for marketing, because there's not as much shared understanding or vocabulary among early adopters. The early ubiquity of Scrum may have limited the ability of Agile software development to think beyond Scrum's parameters. I choose to see the silver lining here and applaud marketers for exploring options for Agility. It means that we all have to speak multiple Agile languages to effectively share our experiences and best practices.

The All-or-Nothing Debate

Many hard-core Scrum practitioners believe that if you haven't adopted 100 percent of Scrum's prescriptions, you can't call yourself Agile. It's a mindset that's proven problematic for members of the development community looking for more flexibility, and it's even harder for new Agile marketers to accept. During the early days of taking her team Agile, Lauren Sozio, former director of product marketing for Skyword, had an immediate negative reaction to all the rigmarole that goes along with Scrum:

> There was no doubt that I found a lot of truth in the agile manifesto, but philosophically, I had a hard time believing that in order to be agile, I had to adopt all ceremonies. This seemed inflexible for a methodology that is grounded in adaptability.[26]

Lauren isn't alone. Many marketers get overwhelmed thinking about everything they'd have to change during an Agile transformation. I hope that thinking outside the Scrum box will help alleviate some of these fears, but if Scrumban and Kanban are still too much for you to consider adopting completely, that doesn't mean Agility is out of your reach.

You can always create a pilot program, either a small sub-team within the department or a single project that you manage using Agile principles, to provide a case study for Agile's viability in your organization. As long as you document your success and commit to expanding your pilots, Agile marketing doesn't have to be an all-or-nothing proposition.

This point will be contested. There are excellent reasons to undertake a wholesale Agile transition for your marketing department, but forcing marketers to choose between being 100 and zero percent Agile does them a disservice. Better to experiment, prove the value, and enjoy a sampling of Agile's many benefits in the short term than wait months or years for sufficient buy-in to flip the Agile switch for the enterprise.

Process Improvement: It's a Marathon, Not a Sprint

No matter what approach you choose, you will not be finished with your adoption this month. Or this quarter. Or this year. Or next year. Agile marketing is a journey whose destination cannot be known or mapped. Just remember that not all who wander are lost.

The tool your team loves right now may become obsolete as you start working on other project types. You may decide to bring in an Agile coach to push you to, and beyond, limits you didn't know were there. A new marketing channel may emerge that destroys your carefully-crafted workflow. The good news? Agile teams prepare for and welcome these changes.

To become one of those teams, you can't slap on Agile as if it were a Band-Aid. You absolutely *must* commit to continuous improvement.

It can be tempting for companies to adopt the language of these concepts but apply them as a veneer on top of their existing ways of working (back to our natural human resistance to change). It's okay to refashion these ideas to better fit your organization. But when doing so, it's worth asking:

What exactly are you going to change about the way
you operate? What are you going to do differently in
your processes, incentives, and decision making that
stands to have a material impact on your business?
What will make tomorrow different from
yesterday?[27]

CHAPTER SEVEN

Understanding the "I" in Agile Teams

"[F]ull-stack marketers are immensely valuable. But they don't come prepackaged from business schools. They're developed through the hands-on practice of agile marketing and democratized innovation. The opportunity to experiment, learn, and grow across a wide spectrum of marketing projects and programs is what produces great full-stack marketers." Scott Brinker, *Hacking Marketing*

These methodologies make *teams* more effective. Solo practitioners can apply some of the foundational principles to enhance their performance, but Agile is rooted in the objective of creating high-functioning teams that can create amazing work.

On the other hand, teams are made up of individual contributors. One bad apple can certainly spoil the barrel on an Agile team just as easily as it can in a more traditionally-structured environment. That means that marketing management must work on two fronts when taking their marketing team Agile. They must look at individual team members as well as team dynamics. The simple solution appears to be to hire a whole bunch of really smart, qualified marketers, teach them a bit about Agility, and turn them loose on a marketing strategy. Like most things about modern marketing, it's not that easy.

Jeff Sutherland tells of a study conducted on students at Yale University. One computer-science course was notoriously hard and the students complained. In response, the professor tracked how long it took each student to complete assignments. A former student then compared that time to the grades each student received, and found no correlation. In fact, the fastest students in the class completed their assignments in one-tenth of the time it took the slowest students, and their grades were just as good.

So it seems that marketing managers should "focus on hiring the quickest people and weeding out the slow-footed," Sutherland wrote. But if you look at teams instead of individuals, the potential for improvement is actually far more dramatic. Citing studies that examined team performance across 3,800 projects of all shapes and sizes, Sutherland reveals:

> If the best team could perform a task in one week, how long do you think it took the worst team?... it took them two *thousand* weeks. That's how great the difference is between the best and worst. So where should you focus your attention? At the level of the individual, where you might be able to get an improvement of ten times if you can magically make all of your employees geniuses? Or at the team level, boosting productivity by an enormous magnitude even if you merely make your worst teams mediocre?[28]

It's not just output that skyrockets when teams become more Agile. The individuals on those teams become more satisfied, loyal, and innovative. It's practically impossible to improve team functionality by focusing exclusively on the people who form the team, but by committing to team improvement through Agility, we change the people within the team.

Agile marketers engage more in their work because they have control over it. Unlike a dictatorial marketing department where contributors simply follow orders, Agile "team members don't have work assigned to them, but instead they take the initiative to accept a new task and commit to completing it" by pulling work from the Backlog.[29] If you're a manager or executive with visions of Agile marketers running amok and working on whatever shiny object catches their eye, fear not. Methodologies provide structure and accountability to the team and its contributors.

While it's true that "marketing executives relinquish more responsibility to agile teams, they retain control over the stories in the backlog and their prioritization. They hold teams accountable for the outcomes of those stories, which are examined at every sprint review, so there's limited room for drift."[30]

Creating a high-functioning team requires deliberate and considered effort, so in this chapter we look at both pieces of the Agile marketing department—the individual marketers and the team they form. A varied skill set is important for a truly Agile marketer, but mindset and attitude matter too. We'll also talk about team size at both extremes, because the challenges of deploying Agile marketing on very small teams and at scale in large departments deserve some attention.

Profile of an Agile Marketer

As in any group, there will be variation among people who practice Agility in marketing, but we can identify some traits, both professional and personal, that contribute to making marketers more successful on an Agile team. Scott Brinker says, "No one on an agile team sits around, waiting for work to be handed to him or her. As part of ownership of their results, team members proactively look for things that need doing and take the initiative to get them done. They pull tasks through the Kanban board. And their flexibility in handling many kinds of tasks, across the different stages in the workflow, means the whole team operates at a high level of utilization."[31]

With that in mind, we can conclude that the best Agile marketers are:

- **T-shaped:** While they have deep expertise in one marketing specialization, they also have a broad, holistic understanding of the marketing field. I've heard more than one marketing manager scoff at the existence of such people, but T-shaped marketers are real. Find as many of them as possible, and keep them around, regardless of cost. They increase your team's agility significantly.

- **Cross-functional:** Closely related to the T-shaped marketer, someone who is cross-functional feels equally comfortable jumping in on an email campaign, giving feedback on social-media content, and writing a blog post. He or she can design a campaign, execute it with a high level of quality, and then analyze and report on the results. It's this wide-ranging skill set that lets him or her chip in on just about any kind of project, which in turn increases an Agile team's velocity.

- **Adaptable:** Having a diverse skill set is useless if you aren't comfortable applying it. Agile marketers are chameleons, moving from situation to situation with little disruption to their output. They often have a well-developed understanding of their own ideal work style and environment and mold each situation to fit their needs.

- **Curious:** Continuous process improvement cannot be undertaken by complacent people. Agile marketers need to be inherently curious. What happens if I change this meeting? How could we engage with our audience a little better? Are we really doing the right work at the right time? They don't break for the sake of breaking, but they are genuinely interested in the results of change.

- **Entrepreneurial:** Agile marketers won't have their work dictated to them. They need to take initiative for forming campaigns and projects based on the stated business value visible in the backlog. An entrepreneurial spirit serves to guide them toward groundbreaking ways of thinking that can improve the team's process and its output.

- **Team-oriented:** Some marketers take Don Draper as their patron saint; they like to swoop in at the last minute with a big idea and save the day. These people find Agile teams difficult, because an Agile environment rewards group success, not personal heroics. As Jeff Sutherland puts it, "A team that depends on regular heroic actions to make its deadlines is not working the way it's supposed to work."[32]

- **Committed to excellence:** Agile marketing is not about pushing substandard work out the door. It's a means to producing better, more effective and impactful marketing. Agile marketers, therefore, must commit fully to producing top-notch work. This doesn't mean they're perfectionists—perfect is the enemy of done, after all—but it *does* mean they want to do the best work possible in the time allotted.

When you're looking to hire new members of your Agile team, keep these characteristics in mind. But what about the people already on your team? The transition to Agility can be tough on some of them, and managers must brace for the occasional casualty when making a dramatic change to how marketing functions. A common behavior in employees who resist Agile marketing structure is information hoarding, a practice that makes them feel more valuable, but in reality, hinders communication and Agility. Teams with these employees must transition them out of the team, "not because they [are] incompetent, but because they [hoard] information and knowledge for their own benefit, to ensure their own indispensibility [sic], rather than helping the team and the company."[33]

You may be surprised who your holdouts are; I've been amazed at the level of personal insult that individuals feel when processes totally unrelated to them are changed. Sergio Zyman reminded me that this kind of reaction isn't unique to an Agile transformation. When he attempted to overhaul marketing departments without any reference to Agile methodologies, he was forced to recognize that "people are comfortable with what's familiar. Some may even personalize this shift, thinking that you are rejecting them along with the old-style marketing."[34]

Remember that while it's deeply team-centric, Agile marketing doesn't work without Agile marketers. You must commit to creating a team that can embrace these ideals and leap into the excitement of uncertainty without hesitation. Then, and only then, do you reap the rewards that Agility has to offer.

The Power of Agile Team Norms

Committed team members put Agile principles into practice daily, but without a supportive environment they have no chance of success, let alone ongoing improvement. "We're *all* creatures of the system we find ourselves embedded in," and if that system is flawed it limits the outcomes even the best teams can achieve.[35]

When Agile systems are given free reign, amazing things can happen. But if lingering flaws in team dynamics continue unchecked, Agile wins die on the vine.

The People Analytics team at Google is tasked with making life at Google "a little bit better and a lot more productive,"[36] and to that end they undertook a massive study of how teams inside Google functioned. Lead by Laszlo Bock, People Operations scoured the literature, interviewed Google employees, and diagrammed the complicated interrelationships between teams. When presenting their findings, Bock reflected, "There's a myth we all carry inside our head. We think we need superstars. But that's not what our research found. You can take a team of average performers, and if you teach them to interact the right way, they'll do things no superstar could ever accomplish."[37]

These "right ways," Bock and his team found, could be summarized in five norms:

1. Teams need to believe their work is important.
2. Teams need to feel their work is personally meaningful.
3. Teams need clear goals and defined roles.
4. Team members need to know they can depend on one another.
5. Most importantly, teams need psychological safety.[38]

All of these norms are necessary on Agile teams to create the optimum environment for true Agility, but psychological safety is the most important. In *The Journal of Applied Behavioral Science*, Amy Edmondson defined the concept as follows:

> Psychological safety is a "shared belief, held by members of a team, that the group is a safe place for taking risks." It is "a sense of confidence that the team will not embarrass, reject, or punish someone for speaking up...It describes a team climate characterized by interpersonal trust and mutual respect in which people are comfortable being themselves."[39]

Imagine a team that enjoys psychological safety conducting a Sprint Retrospective meeting, then imagine the same meeting with a team whose members feel unsafe sharing their thoughts and opinions. Psychological safety not only increases a team's morale and productivity, it's a prerequisite for Agility. Team leaders foster psychological safety and other team-building norms by modeling these behaviors in their own interactions with the team even, and especially, when it would be easy not to do so. In reviewing his exhaustive research on the topic, Duhigg puts it this way:

> There are always good reasons for choosing behaviors that undermine psychological safety. It is often more efficient to cut off debate, to make a quick decision, to listen to whoever knows the most and ask others to hold their tongues. But a team will become an amplification of its internal culture, for better or worse. Study after study shows that while psychological safety might be less efficient in the short run, it's more productive over time.[40]

Agile team members foster psychological safety by sharing control of the team with teammates. We demonstrate that we're actually listening by repeating what someone just said and responding respectfully. If a teammate seems upset, we react with compassion instead of pretending nothing is amiss. By ceding control to the group and consistently displaying our empathy, we create a stronger, more Agile team environment.[41]

Agile Teams Large and Small

People wonder whether Agile marketing works for small teams. The short answer is yes, if you choose the right system.

Don't be intimidated if you have a small team. This can actually be "a powerful advantage, because it enables the maximum amount of harmony across everything that marketing does."[42] A system like Scrum, which is designed to increase visibility within and outside the team, may be too cumbersome for smaller teams, although Jeff Sutherland reports he's seen success with Scrum teams as small as three. My recommendations for teams with under five members is to start with the lighter-weight Kanban methodology, which can enable you to prioritize and execute on separate cadences, with each tied to separate situations and business needs.

If you want to effectively implement Agile marketing on a small team, cross-functionality is crucial. Team members wear many marketing hats, so they need diverse skills to effectively complete projects without relying on outside sources.

If cross-functionality is absent, agencies and freelancers can fill in for the missing skills, but their inclusion can complicate Agile execution. This doesn't mean you can't be agile if you use agencies or freelancers; it means you must pay closer attention to these relationships and how they impact your team's performance. Wherever possible, include freelancers and agency representatives, virtually if necessary, in planning meetings and daily standups. Ratchet up your communication when incorporating people outside the immediate team into Agile marketing work.

Finally, whatever methodology you choose to employ, make sure to avoid overloading the members of your small Agile marketing team. Consider using WIP limits to restrict the number of tasks that each person (including freelancers) can have in progress across the workflow. "This is often helpful when individual team members tend to carry tasks through all the different stages themselves," says Scott Brinker. "They have to focus on completing their current WIP before taking on more."[43]

If you're looking for support in your efforts to be a more Agile marketer on your own, I recommend checking out *Personal Kanban: Mapping Work, Navigating Life* by Tonianne DeMaria Barry and Jim Benson and *Getting Results the Agile Way: A Personal Results System for Work and Life* by J.D. Meier. You can also join the Scrum of One group that I run via TheAgileMarketer.net.

If, on the other hand, you have a large marketing department, you have options for implementing an Agile approach. First, you can choose to create Agile teams under marketing's umbrella and use many of the principles outlined earlier in this section. It's likely that your department is already divided, officially or unofficially, into units, and you can model Agile teams on those existing alignments. When you have a collection of groups like this, you may want to scale by rolling out a meeting called Scrum of Scrums. This technique maintains alignment across Agile teams.

The Scrum of Scrums is a meeting of representatives from all the Scrum teams working on the same project or within one department; it focuses on areas where the teams' work overlaps, integrates, or needs to be handed off. If you had a 30-person marketing department, you might break into five Scrum teams of six members each. Every morning each team would hold their Daily Scrum (Standup) meeting, and then send someone to the Scrum of Scrums meeting. While its purpose is similar to that of the Daily Scrum meeting—to ensure regular and open communication amongst team members that enables work to flow unencumbered—the Scrum of Scrums format may vary slightly.

Mike Cohn, an early innovator in Agile software development, suggests adding a fourth question to the three traditional Standup questions:

1. What has your team done since we last met?
2. What will your team do before we meet again?
3. Is there anything slowing your team down or getting in their way?
4. Are you about to put something in another team's way?[44]

The Scrum of Scrums can be a helpful first step toward scaled Agile marketing, and other Agile methodologies exist to handle the complexities of implementing Agile at scale. These are beyond the scope of this book, but if you hope to expand your Agile marketing implementation beyond two or three core groups of five to ten members, investigate alternative methodologies, including SAFe (Scaled Agile Framework), LeSS (Large Scale Scrum), and DaD (Disciplined Agile Delivery).

CHAPTER EIGHT

Agile Marketing as Competitive Advantage

"If you don't do it, you'll be outsourced. Or your company will die. The hypercompetitive world of twenty-first century work has no room for waste and foolishness." Jeff Sutherland, Scrum[45]

Applying Agile methodologies to marketing is new, but smart marketers have long known the value of taking an Agile approach to their work. From the early days of the digital age to the present, marketing leaders have seen the power of being adaptable, nimble, and iterative while implementing strategy. That the ideals powering Agile marketing are, once seen, so obvious might be why it hasn't already caught fire. Marketers hear the basic concepts of Agility and figure they're already doing most of it:

Of course we need to get regular feedback from our audiences and incorporate it into our next campaign.

Of course we must release smaller pieces more often.

Of course experimentation must be built into our processes.

Smart marketers and smart organizations see the common

sense behind Agile concepts, but most stop there. We experiment, we respond to customer feedback, and we iterate on campaigns. "We already get all the benefits of Agile. Why change how we operate?" But they don't get all the benefits. The real benefits go to organizations that do the work required to change their mindset and their management. These organizations rapidly move ahead of their competition.

Agile Marketing: Winning the Talent Arms Race

The war for marketing talent never ends. "People are the most important factor to marketing's success. Finding, developing, and nurturing great talent is the ultimate source of competitive advantage in modern marketing."[46]

The Agile methodologies that increase a team's productivity also empower the best marketers to do their best work. Agile marketing reduces stress and burnout and brings less-tangible benefits as well. Many head-hunter battles come down to "a competition of passion and imagination. The companies that are best able to stir the minds and souls of the marketers they seek—and give them the powerful organizational platforms on which to achieve great things—will dominate the talent war of modern marketing."[47]

Agile marketing lures potential hires only if they know about it. Spread the word about any Agile transformation your marketing team achieves. Share your story at conferences and meetups, blog about it, contribute to industry publications, and issue a press release. Do whatever it takes to position your marketing team as a place that fosters creativity and values marketers' expertise, a place where Agile lives.

At the turn of the millennium, Sergio Zyman built such a team at Coca-Cola. "You have to create a system and an environment where [the marketers on the team] can flourish and do all of the things that you hired them to do," he wrote in *The End of Marketing as We Know It*. "This means that you have to give them responsibility and authority. You have to trust them...If you provide the environment in which they can test out their dreams, they are going to be eager, energetic, happy, and productive."[48]

By diligently and consciously empowering his team to do their jobs and maintaining expectations of excellence, Zyman propelled Coca-Cola's marketing to its current status. He had an unusual amount of authority to overhaul his team and its approach, but we can achieve the same results without that much pull. The way we structure teams and organizations determines whether we're around in 10 years—or if we'll join the ranks of cautionary tales.

In 1994, James Baron and Michael Hannan, two professors at the Stanford Graduate School of Business, undertook a multiyear study of startups to test an assertion they had long been making to their students: no business survives without a culture of trust among its employees. The flurry of startup companies arising in Silicon Valley provided their petri dish.

Baron and Hannan classified each business in one of five ways:

- **Star model:** Darling of the venture capitalist. Employees come from successful companies or elite schools, and receive high wages and abundant, lavish perks.

- **Engineering model:** Stereotypical start-up. Engineering runs the show. Stars are rare. Programmers pound caffeine and keyboards.

- **Bureaucratic model:** Middle-management culture: job descriptions, org charts, employee handbooks. Regular rituals reinforce company culture.

- **Autocratic model:** Founder or CEO culture. Similar otherwise to the bureaucratic model.

- **Commitment model:** Structured like, but with no cultural similarities to, the bureaucratic model. Employee-first culture to foster employee fulfillment and reciprocal loyalty; fast growth takes a back seat.

Over the next decade, Baron and Hannan watched their startup petri dish companies evolve. Some thrived, others perished. Still others languished somewhere in the middle. But over and over again, the correlation between culture and performance was clear. The star model produced some of the biggest success stories, but firms built on this model also failed in record numbers.

The smart money, it turned out, was on the commitment model. "Hands down, a commitment culture outperformed every other type of management style in almost every meaningful way," with *none* failing during the decade of observation. Employees remained loyal to a culture that valued their contributions, turning down higher-paying jobs elsewhere. "Good employees are always the hardest asset to find," said Baron. "When everyone wants to stick around, you've got a pretty strong advantage." Why doesn't everyone adopt a commitment model?[49]

While developing Scrum, Jeff Sutherland asked the same question. "From day one it was a mystery to me why people insist on working in ways they *know* are inefficient and wasteful and that are dehumanizing and depressing," he wrote.[50] Marketers strangle passion by sticking with models that don't work. To change the outcome, we must change the environment.

Agile marketing can transform your marketing department, making it easier to build and maintain a team that makes marketing magic. But remember, it works the other way too. We're all creatures of the system we find ourselves embedded in; even if you pull together the world's most amazing marketing team, they can still fail spectacularly if your work management methodology hamstrings their efforts. As we learned earlier, you're never really done with Agile. The commitment to continuous improvement has to continue even after you've assembled your marketing dream team.

Organizations that run their marketing teams on Agile principles will attract and retain the best marketing talent. When you combine those people on an Agile team, there's no limit to what they might achieve.

Benefits to the Organization

How do you convince the boss to commit to Agile marketing? This section covers these larger organizational wins from the perspectives of marketing and the organization.

In Wrike's 2016 survey of marketers, they asked marketing users of Agile, "What is the main benefit your team gets from using an Agile process?" The responses:

- Improved quality of work: 18.1 percent
- Faster releases: 16.6 percent
- Better priority alignment: 16.2 percent
- Improved teamwork and morale: 13.7 percent
- Clearer view of project status:13.1 percent
- Faster identification of roadblocks, problems, or schedule issues: 12.6 percent
- Better division of work among team members: 9.7 percent [51]

This survey focused on Agile marketers, but the benefits extend to the top of the marketing food chain.

In a 2014 qualitative study of 40 CMOs, marketing consultancy CMG Partners discovered that while 63 percent of marketing leaders put a high priority on Agility, only 40 percent rated themselves as Agile. The 63 percent were right to prioritize becoming more Agile, because departments who *did* consider themselves Agile were three times as likely to grow market share. In publishing their results on Forbes.com, CMG reported the following business needs that are met with Agility:

In the same article, Barre Hardy, senior director at CMG partners, identified business performance, employee satisfaction, and adaptability as the three biggest upsides to marketing Agility:

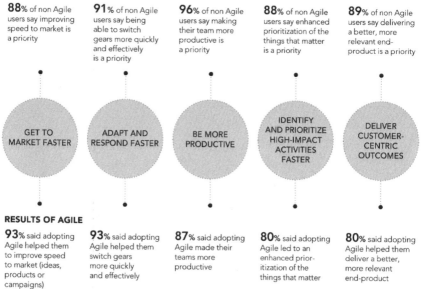

BUSINESS NEEDS

88% of non Agile users say improving speed to market is a priority

91% of non Agile users say being able to switch gears more quickly and effectively is a priority

96% of non Agile users say making their team more productive is a priority

88% of non Agile users say enhanced prioritization of the things that matter is a priority

89% of non Agile users say delivering a better, more relevant end-product is a priority

GET TO MARKET FASTER

ADAPT AND RESPOND FASTER

BE MORE PRODUCTIVE

IDENTIFY AND PRIORITIZE HIGH-IMPACT ACTIVITIES FASTER

DELIVER CUSTOMER-CENTRIC OUTCOMES

RESULTS OF AGILE

93% said adopting Agile helped them to improve speed to market (ideas, products or campaigns)

93% said adopting Agile helped them switch gears more quickly and effectively

87% said adopting Agile made their teams more productive

80% said adopting Agile led to an enhanced prioritization of the things that matter

80% said adopting Agile helped them deliver a better, more relevant end-product

1. **Business Performance:** Agile marketers see increased business performance due to faster delivery, focus on what matters, and greater productivity.

2. **Employee Satisfaction:** Employees working in Agile environments report a greater satisfaction and pride in their work due to feeling more empowered; greater clarity in how their role impacts the business; and a more collaborative work environment.

3. **Adaptability:** Marketers, having built flexibility into their business operations, are better equipped to handle marketplace challenges and opportunities. This is positioning marketing leaders to deliver sustainable growth for their companies.[52]

Agile marketers have the competitive advantage. Scott Brinker: "If you manage through two-week sprints, your management metabolism quickens to 14 days - 543 percent [as fast as] a quarterly rhythm. If a competitor of yours is still slogging along at a quarterly pace, that gives you a 6x advantage over them."[53]

What about (software) teams that have been Agile for over a decade? Here's VersionOne's 2016 "State of Agile Report:"

- 87 percent: Ability to manage changing priorities
- 85 percent: Increased team productivity
- 84 percent improved project visibility
- 81 percent increased team morale/motivation
- 81 percent better deliverability predictability [54]

If you start your Agile journey now, these benefits could apply to your marketing team and your organization next year.

Maintaining Strategic Alignment

The day-to-day grind of keeping the marketing machine running often obscures the larger marketing strategies and business goals—the reasons for writing all those blog posts and sending all those Tweets. Agile marketing, with its regular pauses for planning and reprioritization, can be the cure for this strategic blindness.

Whether you use Scrum Sprints or Kanban cadences, each release cycle on an Agile marketing team is like a bicycle wheel: each spin of the wheel brings the cyclist closer to her goal. "But strategy," says Brinker, "is applied with the handlebars, pointing the bicycle in the right direction. Pedaling (execution) and steering (strategy) work together to get us to our direction (vision)."[55]

Some teams divide their visual board into horizontal rows—swim lanes—that correspond to strategic themes or long-term goals, an arrangement that makes it easier to track progress toward each objective.[56] Regardless of the technique they use, Agile teams find it easier to keep tactics in sync with strategy.

The Cure for the 50-Hour Work Week

Remember Part Two when we learned that marketers work an average of 45.9 hours per week? Besides disrupting your work-life balance, those extra hours reduce your productivity. When Scott Maxwell implemented Scrum across the organization at OpenView Venture Partners, he was taking on a typical high-powered culture. There was the "expectation that people would work late and on the weekends. These were aggressive, ambitious people. But they were getting burned out, depressed, and demoralized."[57] We can make only so many decisions in a day before we erode our ability to regulate our behavior. We make mistakes, eventually serious mistakes, and our productivity plummets.

Going home at five o'clock isn't a sign of laziness or a lack of commitment. It's a sign that you get stuff done. Agile supports this mindset. "Hours themselves represent a cost," Sutherland argues. "Instead, measure *output*. Who cares how many hours someone worked on something? All that matters is how fast it's delivered and how good it is."[58]

"But," I can hear you say, "my team needs me to work this many hours. If I don't swoop in and save the day, nothing gets done." It might make you feel heroic in the moment, but teams that routinely rely on this kind of Don Draper-esque rescue aren't high-functioning. Taiichi Ohno, a pioneering Agile thinker from Toyota, classifies this behavior as a type of waste that Agile teams must eliminate. Ohno calls it "Unreasonableness," a category that includes absurd goals, unrealistic expectations, and overburdened team members. If your team operates under the weight of any of these, neither individuals nor department are working to their highest potential. Existing from one crisis to the next isn't living; that's as true in a professional context as it is in your personal life.

There's no need to settle for a career of fire drills. Pour some Agility on that fire and go to work.

Bringing Marketing Back to Life

None of us has more than 24 hours in a day. No marketing department, no matter how large or well funded, can add more time to a day, a week, or a quarter. It's easy to pass the buck, saying that your boss, your VP, or your CMO won't let you change how you spend your time. It's easy to stay locked into the way you've been working for years.

However, the history of marketing is the story of those who shun what is easy in favor of what is great. After decades of gradual, cyclical progression, our profession is moving forward with unprecedented speed.

Marketing employees, teams, and organizations can choose to operate in a vacuum, ignore our predecessors and the winds of change, and lose the innovation arms race. Let's not. Let's step out on the road less traveled by reclaiming the precious time that makes up our days. Our lives are made of nothing but time; squandering it is slow suicide.

Marketing matters. It has always mattered. Perhaps more importantly, individual marketers matter. Agile walls can protect us from the mindless, soulless, meaningless trivia of rote tasks that create the worst kind of work. We have to put in the effort to raise those walls and start to resuscitate a meaningful profession.

Citations

Part 1

1. Fox, Stephen, *The Mirror Makers: A History of American Advertising & Its Creators* (Champaign: University of Illinois Press, 1997). p306
2. Cluley, Robert , (2016),"The depiction of marketing and marketers in the news media ", *European Journal of Marketing*, Vol. 50 Iss 5/6 p. 753
3. Fox, *The Mirror Makers*, p6.
4. Quoted in The Mirror Makers, p108.
5. Tungate, Mark, *Adland: A Global History of Advertising*, 2nd edition (Philadelphia: Kogan Page Limited, 2013).
6. Ibid, pp 7-8
7. Acunzo, Jay, "The History of Advertising: How Consumers Won the War for Their Attention," July 1, 2013. https://blog.hubspot.com/marketing/the-history-of-advertising-war-for-consumer-attention-slideshare#sm.000 01v2x90g6budzvu254ffpgua2s
8. Acunzo, slide 58.
9. Magazines.com, "History of Magazines," Accessed December 28, 2016. https://www.magazines.com/history-of-magazines
10. "History of Magazine Publishing," http://open.lib.umn.edu/mediaandculture/chapter/5-2-history-of-magazine-publishing/
11. Douglas, Torin, *The Complete Guide to Advertising*, (London:

Macmillan, 1984).

12. Godin, Seth, *Meatball Sundae: Is Your Marketing Out of Sync?* (New York: Penguin Books, 2007). pp 33-39

13. Hagley Museum and Library, "History of Patent Medicine," Accessed December 28, 2016. http://www.hagley.org/online_exhibits/patentmed/history/history.html

14. Fox, *The Mirror Makers*, p17.

15. Fox, *The Mirror Makers*, p15.

16. *Advertising Age*, "Ad Age Advertising Century: Top 100 People - John E. Powers", Published March 29, 1999; accessed December 28, 2016. http://adage.com/article/special-report-the-advertising-century/john-e-powers/140264/

17. Fox, *The Mirror Makers*, p71.

18. Tungate, *Adland*, p13.

19. Fox, *The Mirror Makers*, p71.

20. Ibid, p65.

21. Ibid, p66.

22. Ibid, p67.

23. Ibid, p77.

24. Kisseloff, Jeff, *The Box: An Oral History of Television, 1929-1961* (New York: Penguin Books, 1997). p 499

25. Tungate, *Adland*, 29

26. Fox, *The Mirror Makers*, p95

27. Ibid, p117.

28. Ibid, p97.

29. Ibid, p119

30. Ibid, p120.

31. Tungate, *Adland*, p25.

32. Fox, *The Mirror Makers*, p120.

33. Ibid.

34. Ibid, p168.

35. Tungate, *Adland*, p31.

36. McConnell, Ben and Jackie Huba, *Citizen Marketers: When People Are the Message* (Chicago: Kaplan Publishing, 2007). p74

37. Sarnoff, David, "Probable Influences of Television on

Society," *Journal of Applied Physics*, July, 1939.
38. Kisseloff, *The Box*, p50.
39. Ponce de Leon, Charles L, *That's the Way it Is: A History of Television News in America* (Chicago: The University of Chicago Press, 2015). p14
40. Ibid, p16.
41. Ibid, p17.
42. Kisseloff, *The Box*, 143.
43. Ibid.
44. Ibid, p52.
45. Ibid, pp101-102.
46. Booker, M. Keith and Bob Batchelor, *Mad Men: A Cultural History* (New York: Rowman & Littlefield Publishers, 2016).
47. Fox, *The Mirror Makers*, p173.
48. Booker and Batchelor, *Mad Men*, introduction
49. Fox, *The Mirror Makers*, p179.
50. Ibid, pp179-180.
51. Ibid, p200.
52. Ibid, p209.
53. Ibid, p177.
54. Tungate, *Adland*, p4.
55. Booker and Batchelor, *Mad Men*, p32.
56. Cluley, Robert, "Depictions of Marketers," p754.
57. Ibid.
58. Booker and Batchelor, *Mad Men*, pp212-213.
59. Fox, *The Mirror Makers*, p218.
60. Tungate, *Adland*, p95
61. Booker and Batchelor, *Mad Men*, p198.
62. Ibid, p42.
63. Fox, *The Mirror Makers*, p229.
64. Ibid, p324.
65. Mayer, Martin, *Whatever Happened to Madison Avenue? Advertising in the '90s* (New York: Little Brown & Co, 1991). p3
66. Fox, *The Mirror Makers*, pii
67. Strangelove, Michael, *Post-TV: Piracy, Cord-Cutting and the Future of Television* (Toronto: University of Toronto Press, 2015). p207

68. Ibid, p22.
69. Ibid, p28.
70. Kisseloff, *The Box*, p300.

Part 2

1. Tungate, Mark, *Adland: A Global History of Advertising*, 2nd edition (Philadelphia: Kogan Page Limited, 2013). p251
2. Fox, Stephen, *The Mirror Makers: A History of American Advertising & Its Creators* (Champaign: University of Illinois Press, 1997). p53
3. Vaynerchuk, Gary, *Jab, Jab, Jab, Right Hook: How to Tell Your Story in a Noisy Social World* (New York: Harper Collins, 2013). p4
4. Ibid, pp187-188.
5. http://www.nytimes.com/2016/01/31/business/media/meredith-wild-a-self-publisher-making-an-imprint.html?_r=0
6. http://www.journalism.org/2016/06/15/podcasting-fact-sheet/
7. McConnell, Ben and Jackie Huba, *Citizen Marketers: When People Are the Message* (Chicago: Kaplan Publishing, 2007). pvii
8. http://www.davecarrollmusic.com/songwriting/united-breaks-guitars/
9. https://www.theguardian.com/news/blog/2009/jul/23/youtube-united-breaks-guitars-video
10. McConnell and Huba, *Citizen Marketers*, p77
11. Anderson, Chris, *The Longer Long Tail: How Endless Choice is Creating Unlimited Demand* (New York : Random House Business, 2009). pp 56-57
12. Ibid, p52
13. Godin, Seth, *Meatball Sundae: Is Your Marketing Out of Sync?* (New York: Penguin Books, 2007). p47
14. Zyman, Sergio, *The End of Marketing As We Know It* (New York: HarperBusiness, 2000). p102
15. Anderson, *The Longer Long Tail*, p53
16. Ibid, p54

17. Kisseloff, Jeff, *The Box: An Oral History of Television, 1929-1961* (New York: Penguin Books, 1997). p143
18. Anderson, *The Longer Long Tail*, p99
19. Fox, Stephen, *The Mirror Makers: A History of American Advertising & Its Creators* (Champaign: University of Illinois Press, 1997). p71
20. Godin, *Meatball Sundae*, pp192-193.
21. Anderson, *The Longer Long Tail*, p63
22. Godin, *Meatball Sundae*, pp xii-xiii
23. Ibid, p23.
24. Ibid, p48.
25. Ibid, p15.
26. Tungate, *Adland*, p198.
27. *New Media Age*, "How dotcoms killed off the ad agencies," September 13, 2011.
28. "Study of Dot-Com Marketing Finds Major Improvements" http://adage.com/article/digital/study-dot-marketing-finds-major-improvements/37286/
29. Tungate, *Adland*, p199.
30. Mieszkowski, Katharine, "Fumble.com" May 2, 2000. http://www.salon.com/2000/05/03/super_ads/
31. Study by D'Arcy Masius Benton & Bowles - DMBB
32. Tungate, *Adland*, p15.
33. Godin, *Meatball Sundae*, p217.
34. Zyman, *End of Marketing*, p180.
35. McConnell and Huba, *Citizen Marketers*, pvii-ix.
36. Zyman, *End of Marketing*, p179
37. Williams, Bri, "Anyone can be a marketer," June 11, 2014. https://www.marketingmag.com.au/hubs-c/anyone-can-be-a-marketer/
38. Zyman, *End of Marketing*, pp179-180.
39. Ibid, 180.
40. http://theaccidentalmarketer.com/
41. Spitale, Tom and Mary Abbazia, *The Accidental Marketer: Power Tools for People Who Find Themselves in Marketing Roles* (New York: Wiley, 2014). p197
42. https://www.fournaisegroup.com/ceos-do-not-trust-marketers/

43. https://www.fournaisegroup.com/marketers-lack-credibility/
44. https://www.fournaisegroup.com/ceos-do-not-trust-marketers/
45. Fox, *The Mirror Makers*, p179
46. Ibid, p314.
47. Ibid, p327.
48. Facebook, "Form S-1 Registration Statement: Facebook, Inc.," February 1, 2012. www.sec.gov/Archives/edgar/data/1326801/000119312512034517/d28795ds1.htm
49. Acunzo, Jay, "Confessions of a Content Creator: I Don't Care About Data," June 3, 2016. http://unthinkable.fm/hubris-of-data-driven-thinking/
50. Cluley, Robert, (2016), "The depiction of marketing and marketers in the news media," *European Journal of Marketing*, Vol. 50 Iss 5/6 p. 753.
51. Van Praet, Douglas. "How Marketers Manipulate You Without You Knowing." June 3, 2013. https://www.psychologytoday.com/blog/unconscious-branding/201306/how-marketers-manipulate-you-without-your-knowing
52. Cluley, "The depiction of marketing and marketers in the news media," p765
53. Ibid, p763
54. Ibid.
55. Dowling, Finnegan, "A Full Disclosure Blog: Three Reasons You DON'T Want to Adopt Eddie The Terrible." December 9, 2014. http://hssvacc.blogspot.com/2014/12/a-full-disclosure-blog-three-reasons.html
56. Handley, Ann. "Creative, Funny, Unusually Honest Marketing of an Awful Dog Named 'Eddie the Terrible'" December 16, 2014. http://www.annhandley.com/2014/12/16/eddie-the-terrible-ridiculously-good-writing/
57. 2016-2017 State of Enterprise Work Report: U.S. Edition. https://resources.workfront.com/workfront-awareness/2016-state-of-enterprise-work-report-u-s-edition

Part 3

1. The Agile Marketing Manifesto. http:// agilemarketingmanifesto.org/; accessed January 4, 2017.
2. Brinker, Scott, *Hacking Marketing: Agile Practices to Make Marketing Smarter, Faster, and More Innovative.* (Hoboken: John Wiley & Sons, Inc.: 2016). p56
3. Sutherland, Jeff and J.J. Sutherland, *Scrum: The Art of Doing Twice the Work in Half the Time* (New York: Crown Business, 2014). p19.
4. Ibid, p8
5. "The Scrum Guide" http://www.scrumguides.org/docs/ scrumguide/v1/scrum-guide-us.pdf, accessed January 4, 2017.
6. Ibid.
7. Sutherland, *Scrum*, p71.
8. Ibid, pp78-79.
9. http://www.retrospectives.com/pages/ retroPrimeDirective.html, accessed January 4, 2017.
10. Brinker, *Hacking Marketing*, p83.
11. Ibid, p133.
12. Anderson, David J., *Kanban: Successful Evolutionary Change for Your Technology Business*, (Sequim, Washington: Blue Hole Press, 2010). p27.
13. Ibid, p34.
14. Ibid, p39.
15. Brinker, *Hacking Marketing*, p107.
16. Anderson, *Kanban*, p105.
17. Ibid, p106.
18. Reddy, Ajay, *The Scrumban [R]Evolution: Getting the Most Out of Agile, Scrum, and Lean Kanban* (Crawfordsville, Indiana: Pearson Education, 2016) p16.
19. Reddy, *The Scrumban [R]Evolution*, p273.
20. Ries, Eric, *The Lean Startup: How Today's Entrepreneurs Use Continuous Innovation to Create Radically Successful Businesses* (New York: Crown Publishing Group, 2011).
21. http://www.lean.org/whatslean/principles.cfm, accessed January 4, 2017.

22. https://blog.hubspot.com/blog/tabid/6307/bid/33718/
    Lean-Marketing-How-to-Run-Your-Marketing-Team-Like-
    a-Startup.aspx#sm.00001v2x90g6budzvu254ffpgua2s,
    accessed December 29, 2016.
23. http://stateofagile.versionone.com/, accessed January 3,
    2017
24. https://www.workfront.com/resources/ebook/agile-
    marketing-report-2016/, accessed January 2, 2017.
25. https://www.wrike.com/library/ebooks/agile-marketing-
    report-2016/, accessed January 2, 2017.
26. https://www.skyword.com/contentstandard/marketing/
    when-agile-marketing-goes-overboard-and-how-to-reel-it-
    in/, accessed December 30, 2016.
27. Brinker, *Hacking Marketing*, p53.
28. Sutherland, *Scrum*, p42
29. Brinker, *Hacking Marketing*, p112.
30. Ibid, p135.
31. Ibid, p132.
32. Sutherland, *Scrum*, p107.
33. Sutherland, *Scrum*, p142.
34. Zyman, Sergio, *The End of Marketing As We Know It* (New
    York: HarperBusiness, 2000). p50.
35. Sutherland, *Scrum*, p65.
36. Duhigg, Charles, *Smarter Faster Better: The Secrets to Being
    Productive in Life and Business* (New York: Penguin Random
    House, 2016). p42.
37. Ibid, p65.
38. Ibid, p66.
39. Ibid, p50
40. Ibid, p69.
41. Ibid, p70.
42. Brinker, *Hacking Marketing*, p130.
43. Ibid, p111.
44. https://www.scrumalliance.org/community/
    articles/2007/may/advice-on-conducting-the-scrum-of-
    scrums-meeting, accessed January 3, 2017.
45. Sutherland, *Scrum* p20.
46. Brinker, *Hacking Marketing*, p249.

47. Ibid, p250.

48. Zyman, *The End of Marketing*, pp186-187.

49. Duhigg, *Smarter Faster Better*, pp145-150.

50. Sutherland, *Scrum*, p28.

51. https://www.wrike.com/library/ebooks/agile-marketing-report-2016/, accessed December 28, 2016.

52. http://www.forbes.com/sites/jenniferrooney/2014/04/15/applying-agile-methodology-to-marketing-can-pay-dividends-survey/#524adbe9391e, accessed January 2, 2017.

53. Brinker, *Hacking Marketing*, pp76-77.

54. http://stateofagile.versionone.com/

55. Brinker, *Hacking Marketing*, p146.

56. Ibid, p148.

57. Sutherland, *Scrum*, p102.

58. Ibid, p105.

Acknowledgments

I'm someone who works independently most of the time (and likes it that way). But bringing a project like this into the world is not a one-woman show. And so, I need to thank:

Dan Partain, my husband and tireless advocate. Thank you for keeping the kids out of my office for ten days while I wrote nonstop, for keeping me on a (relatively) even keel, and listening to me talk about David Ogilvy and measuring throughput in the same breath.

My sweet son Brennan. You can't read this just yet, but when you asked me to read you my book, and then sat and listened to a whole five pages before getting bored, it was amazing. Thank you.

My parents, Ken and Cindy Fryrear. Thanks for letting me read all the time when I was a kid, for letting me get a degree in English (see! It does have real world applications!) instead of Engineering, and generally being the world's greatest parents.

Ray Johnston, my first (and most ruthless) editor. Everybody should be lucky enough to have someone like you working on their book. Thank you for caring about the end result so much, and for reminding me that more adjectives aren't always a good thing.

Anthony Coppedge. Thank you for continually reminding me why this topic matters, and for keeping me true to both myself and Agile ideals. You're a rare find, my friend.

Jeff Julian. Thanks for being an enthusiastic voice when I was taking my first tentative Agile steps and always bringing the coolest gadgets to conferences.

The super smart and welcoming Agile marketing community. Scott Brinker, John Cass, Frank Days, Roland Smart, Barre Hardy, Raechel Duplain, David Lesue, Jascha Kaykas-Wolff, Jeff Julian, and so many more -- you all make it fun and challenging and exciting to work in this field. Thank you for everything you contribute!

Susie Schaefer and My Word Publishing. How on earth would I have gotten all of this done without you?! Thank you for appearing in the nick of time and saving me from developing a drinking problem in the weeks leading up to publication.

The Content Marketing Institute, specifically Michele Linn, Marcia Reifer-Johnston, Clare McDermott, Joe Pulizzi, and Robert Rose. Thank you for seeing the value of Agile for content marketing and letting me share these ideas through the CMI blog, at Content Marketing World, and at the Intelligent Content Conference.

My good friends at Workfront, Scott Duehlmeier, Heather Hurst, Raechel DuPlain, Marcus Varner, Dave Lesué, and Joe Staples. Thank you all for trusting me with multiple blog posts, webinars, and presentations on Agile marketing, and for being believers in the Agile way.

Christian Vanek, Josh Robitaille, and the marketing team at SurveyGizmo. Thanks for giving me leeway to chase this whole Agile thing, and for going along with my crazy experiments.

About the Author

Andrea is the President and Lead Trainer for AgileSherpas, a training, education, and consulting company designed to help marketers transform the way they work. Her formal agile qualifications include Certified Professional in Agile Coaching (ICP-ACC), Certified Agile Leader (CAL-1), Certified Agile Marketer (ICP-MKG), and ICAgile Authorized Instructor. She is a sought-after international speaker on the intersections of agility and marketing, having appeared at Content Marketing World, SXSW, The Intelligent Content Conference, MarketingProfs B2B Marketing Forum, MarTech San Francisco, and The Business Agility Conference to name a few. In *Death of a Marketer* she combines more than a fourteen years of digital marketing expertise with thorough research and in-the-trenches agile experience. Her pet peeves include misuse of quotation marks and running out of wine when on deadline. If she's not attending a Standup meeting or facilitating Retrospective, she's almost certainly on a volleyball court somewhere.

Let's Get Agile

Ah, marketing.

When it's good, it's singing, dancing, kittens, and rainbows good. And when it's bad, it's mind-numbingly, soul-crushingly bad.

My partner and I started AgileSherpas because we discovered that Agile marketing is a way to help marketing teams spend more time dancing with kittens and less time regretting our career choices.

Agile teams do better work in less time with less stress. What's not to love? Change. Change is what most of us don't love.

Agile marketing represents a huge change in how marketers have historically managed their work, and we get it — change is hard. Through education, training, and coaching, AgileSherpas is here to make this one easier. We strive to be Sherpas in the true sense of the word, guiding you along the path towards greater agility while always on the lookout for new and better routes.

If you're ready to start on this amazing journey, we'd be honored to join you. Everyone's path is different, so we have online courses, in-person workshops, customized trainings, and long-term coaching available to get you moving in the right direction, and helping you reach your desired destination.

Here are a few of our most popular options. Find more at AgileSherpas.com.

Online Course: Introduction to Agile Marketing

Marketing exists in a state of constant change. New channels emerge overnight, audiences expect perfectly targeted messaging, there are never quite enough resources to go around, and marketing technology just keeps getting more complex. And yet marketers aren't evolving to keep up with all this change. We use outdated methods to manage our work (if we have any work management system in place at all). We live with inefficiencies and stress, assuming that's just the way that marketing is.

Fellow marketers, there's a better way to work.

In this 80-minute course Andrea Fryrear will introduce you to the next great stage in marketing evolution: Agile marketing.

What You'll Learn

- Why Agile you should be embracing Agile marketing NOW, and how its roots in software development make it the perfect fit for modern marketing.

- What Agile marketing really is, and, just as importantly, what it isn't.

- How Agile marketing benefits everyone in an organization, from the newest digital marketing specialist to executive leadership to the customers we serve.

- Who should be using Agile marketing, including the marketing functions that are best suited for an Agile marketing trial.

- How to deal with the challenges of large and small marketing teams, as well as those that rely on agencies and freelancers to complete their work.

- An introduction to how you apply Agile principles to marketing work using the three most common Agile methodologies: Scrum, Kanban, and Scrumban.

- Tips for getting started on your Agile adoption that will give your team the best chance for a successful Agile transformation.

  https://agilesherpas.thinkific.com/courses/introduction-to-agile-marketing

Agile Marketing Fundamentals

Using a combination of lecture and hands-on activities, this 2-day in-person workshop will provide everything you need to start practicing Agile marketing with confidence.

From choosing the right methodology to avoiding common pitfalls, our expert Agile Sherpas will set you on the path to a more effective, more efficient, more Agile way of marketing.

Who should attend this workshop?

You can attend individually or as team. We've designed this workshop to serve:

- Stressed out marketers looking for ways to get more done in less time
- Marketing teams who want a better way to connect with their audiences & customers
- Agile skeptics who aren't sure these practices work in marketing
- Marketing agencies looking to deliver more value to their clients
- Any marketing professional who's ever thought, "There's got to be a better way to do this."

What You'll Learn

- Why Agile is the answer to marketing challenges like rising audience expectations, exploding channel complexity, ever more sophisticated marketing technology.

- What Agile marketing really is, and, just as importantly, what it isn't.

- How Agile marketing helps keep your team constantly focused on customers and their needs.

- Three core Agile methodologies — Scrum, Kanban, and Scrumban — and when to apply each one.

- How to create a culture of validated learning on your marketing team, from incremental improvement to iterative expansion.

- The Agile approach to collaboration, alignment, and setting up effective teams.

All who complete this workshop will become Certified Professionals in Agile Marketing, the first ever Agile Marketing Certification through ICAgile, the international certification and accreditation body.